Contents

Contents

Name _____

Strategy Workshop

As you listen to the story "The Rule," by Anne Cameron, you will stop from time to time to do some activities on these practice pages. These activities will help you think about different strategies that can help you read better. After completing each activity, you will discuss what you've written with your classmates and talk about how to use these strategies.

Remember, strategies can help you become a better reader. Good readers

- use strategies whenever they read

- use different strategies before, during, and after reading

- think about how strategies will help them

Name _____

Strategy 1: Predict/Infer

Use this strategy before and during reading to help make predictions about what happens next or what you're going to learn.

Here's how to use the Predict/Infer strategy:

1. Think about the title, the illustrations, and what you have read so far.
2. Tell what you think will happen next—or what you will learn. Thinking about what you already know about the subject may help.
3. Try to figure out things the author does not say directly.

Listen as your teacher begins "The Rule." When your teacher stops, complete the activity with a partner to show that you understand how to predict what you think might happen in the story.

Think about the story and respond to the question below.

What do you think might happen in the story?

_____

_____

As you continue listening to the story, think about whether your prediction was right. You might want to change your prediction or write a new one below.

_____

_____

Name _____

Strategy 2: Phonics/Decoding

Use this strategy during reading when you come across a word you don't know.

Here's how to use the Phonics/Decoding strategy:

1. Look carefully at the word.
2. Look for word parts that you know and think about the sounds for the letters.
3. Blend the sounds to read the word.
4. Ask yourself if this is a word you know and whether the word makes sense in the sentence.
5. If not, ask yourself if there is anything else you could try—should you look in the dictionary?

Listen as your teacher continues to read the story. When your teacher stops, use the Phonics/Decoding strategy.

Now write down the steps you used to decode the word *trout*.

_____

_____

_____

_____

_____

_____

_____

Remember to use this strategy whenever you are reading and come across a word that you don't know.

Name _____

Strategy 3: Monitor/Clarify

Use this strategy during reading whenever you're confused about what you are reading.

Here's how to use the Monitor/Clarify strategy:

- Ask yourself if what you're reading makes sense—or if you are learning what you need to learn.
- If you don't understand something, reread, look at the illustrations, or read ahead to see if that helps.

Listen as your teacher continues to read the story. When your teacher stops, complete the activity with a partner to show that you understand how to figure out why the boy in the story might think the mushrooms look like a forest.

Think about the story and respond below.

1. Have you ever eaten mushrooms? What do they look like?

_____

_____

2. Can you tell from listening to the story why the boy may have thought the mushrooms looked like a forest? Why or why not?

_____

_____

3. How can you find out why he may have thought that?

_____

_____

Name _____

Strategy 4: Question

Use this strategy during and after reading to ask questions about important ideas in the story.

Here's how to use the Question strategy:

- Ask yourself questions about important ideas in the story.
- Ask yourself if you can answer these questions.
- If you can't answer the questions, reread and look for answers in the text. Thinking about what you already know and what you've read in the story may help you.

Listen as your teacher continues to read the story. Then complete the activity with a partner to show that you understand how to ask yourself questions about important ideas in the story.

Think about the story and respond below.

Write a question you might ask yourself at this point in the story.

_____

_____

_____

_____

_____

If you can't answer your question now, think about it while you listen to the rest of the story.

Name _____

Strategy 5: Evaluate

Use this strategy during and after reading to help you form an opinion about what you read.

Here's how to use the Evaluate strategy:
- Think about how the author makes the story come alive and makes you want to read it.
- Think about what was entertaining, informative, or useful about the selection.
- Think about how you reacted to the story—how well you understood the selection and whether you enjoyed reading it.

Listen as your teacher continues to read the story. When your teacher stops, complete the activity with a partner to show that you are thinking of how you feel about what you are reading and why you feel that way.

Think about the story and respond below.

1. Tell whether or not you think this story is entertaining and why.

_____

_____

2. This is a humorous, realistic fiction story. Did the author make the characters interesting and believable?

_____

_____

3. How did you react to this story?

_____

Name _____

Strategy 6: Summarize

Use this strategy after reading to summarize what you read.

Here's how to use the Summarize strategy:
- Think about the characters.
- Think about where the story takes place.
- Think about the problem in the story and how the characters solve it.
- Think about what happens in the beginning, middle, and end of the story.

Think about the story you just listened to. Complete the activity with a partner to show that you understand how to identify important story parts that will help you summarize the story.

Think about the story and respond to the questions below:

1. Who is the main character?

_____

_____

2. Where does the story take place?

_____

_____

3. What is the problem and how is it resolved?

_____

_____

Now use this information to summarize the story for a partner.

Name _____

Off to Adventure!

Cut out a picture of something you think is an adventure from a magazine or a newspaper. Paste it on this page. Then answer the questions below.

1. What do you think makes this an adventure?

_____

_____

2. How would you describe this adventure to someone?

_____

_____

3. Would you like to be part of this adventure? Explain your answer.

_____

_____

Off to Adventure!

As you read each selection in *Off to Adventure!*, fill in the
boxes of the chart that apply to the selection.

	How does the adventure begin?	How do the characters change by the end of the adventure?
The Lost and Found		
The Ballad of Mulan		
The Waterfall		

Name _____

What a Day!

Joey has just moved to a new town. Help him finish a letter to his friend. Fill in the blanks with the correct words from the box.

Vocabulary

rumpled
situations
worried
visible
unusual
directions

September 5

Dear Flora:

My first day of school was full of unlucky

_____. I wanted to wear my favorite

shirt, but it was all _____ from being

packed in a box. While I was looking for something else to

wear, I missed the bus. My parents drove me to school, but we

got lost on the way. We had to stop and ask for

_____. I was _____

that I would be late for school, but we got there just in time.

At noon, I couldn't find my lunchbox. I looked everywhere,

but it wasn't _____. Then my day got

better. Some nice students asked me to sit with them. They

shared their lunches with me. It was an _____ way

to make new friends, but I'm glad it happened!

Your friend,

Joey

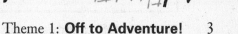

Theme 1: **Off to Adventure!**   3

Name _____

Event Map

Pages 20–21

Wendell and Floyd are at the principal's office. Then Mona

enters and says _____

_____

Page 23

Mona leans so far into the bin that only her feet are showing.

A moment later, _____

Pages 26–27

The boys _____

Pages 30–31

The children see a sign to the Hat Room, so they follow a

passageway to _____

Pages 34–37

The children come to a hallway lined with doors. Finally, Mona opens

one last door and finds _____

Name _____

Tell the True Story

The underlined part of each sentence below is false.
Rewrite it as a true sentence about *The Lost and Found*.

1. Wendell and Floyd are waiting to see the principal because they missed <u>their bus.</u>

   _____

   _____

2. Mona walks into the office to <u>borrow some lunch money.</u>

   _____

   _____

3. The boys want to climb into the Lost and Found bin to <u>get away from a giant squid.</u>

   _____

   _____

4. The children cross the lake to find <u>the school library.</u>

   _____

   _____

5. In the Hat Room, the boys start <u>looking for their lost baseball caps.</u>

   _____

   _____

6. Mona finds her lucky hat <u>hanging on the Hat Room door.</u>

   _____

   _____

Name _____

Story Events

Read the story. Think about what happens. Then fill in the chart on the next page.

Surprise!

After a long drive, Mom, Dad, and I got to Golden Lake. We were tired, so we set up camp and climbed into our sleeping bags. Then I said, "I hate camping. Why did you make me come?"

"You never know what can happen, Jenny," Dad answered. "You could be in for a big surprise!"

The next morning, I couldn't believe my eyes. There, sitting by the tent was a bee the size of an airplane! "Hop on!" shouted Dad over its loud hum. "Come for a ride."

We all got onto the bee's big, fuzzy back. Then it lifted off. It zoomed right and left. It sailed over the water and made loops in the air. What a fun ride!

At last, the bee landed by our camp. We all climbed off. Then it flew away. I stood there with my mouth open. Dad smiled and said, "Just wait until tomorrow's surprise!"

Name _____

Story Events continued

Fill in the blanks to tell what happened in the story.

The family sets up camp at Golden Lake.

↓

Jenny says she hates camping, but Dad tells her she may be in for a surprise.

↓

The next morning _____

↓

The family climbs onto its back.

↓

Then the bee _____

↓

At last the bee _____

↓

The family climbs off.

↓

The bee _____

Name _____

Base Words

Some words are formed from a **base word,** a word that can stand by itself. In the word *climbing*, the base word is *climb*. Letters can be added to the beginning or the end of a base word, as you see here.

appear / **dis**appear   boat / boat**er**   turn / turn**ed**

Some of the words in this Lost and Found bin contain base words. Circle the base word in those words. Then write each base word on the lines below.

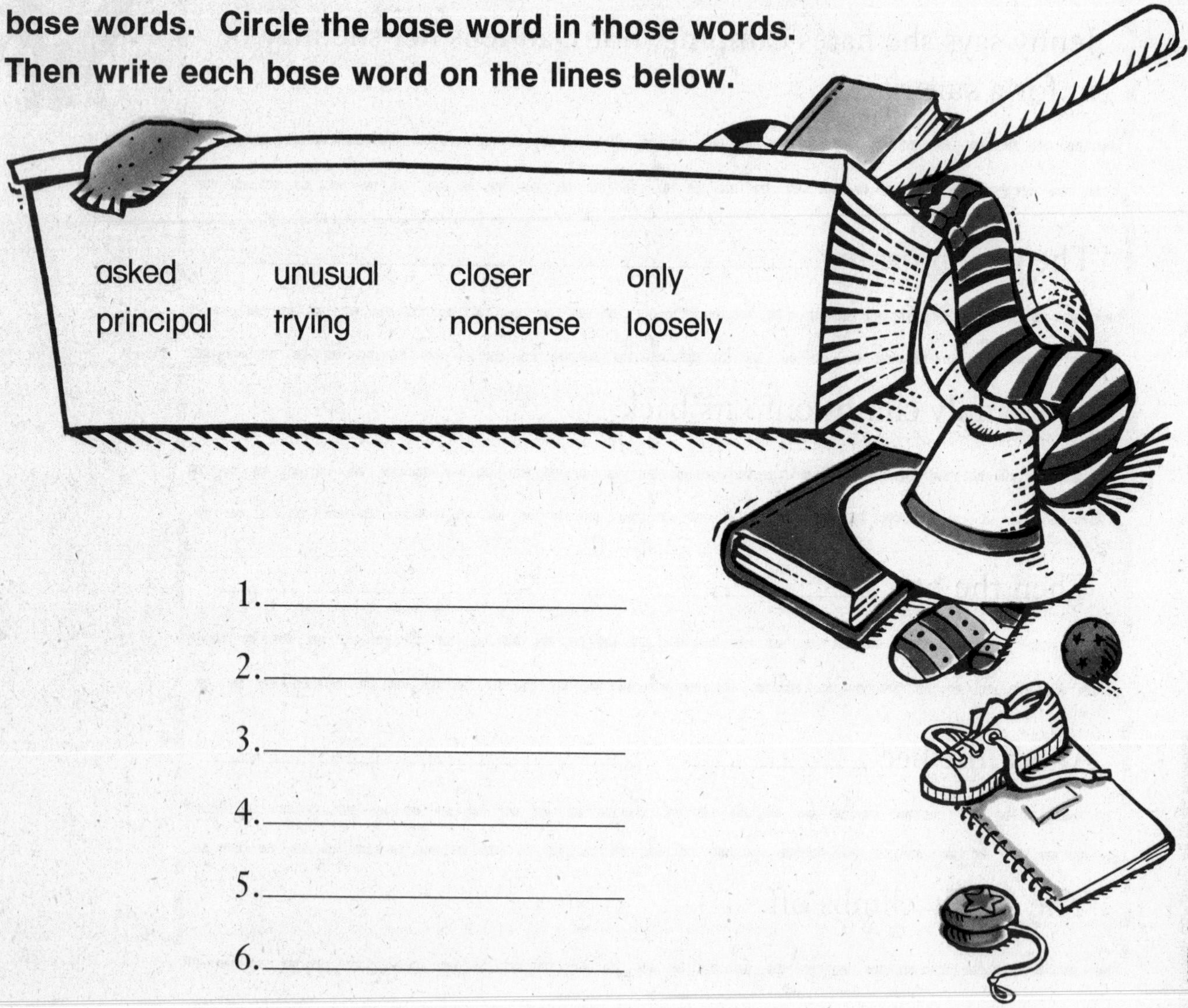

asked	unusual	closer	only
principal	trying	nonsense	loosely

1._____

2._____

3._____

4._____

5._____

6._____

Name _____

Short Vowels

► A short vowel sound is usually spelled with one vowel followed by a consonant sound.

The /ă/ sound is usually spelled **a,** as in la**s**t.

The /ĕ/ sound is usually spelled **e,** as in sm**e**ll.

The /ĭ/ sound is usually spelled **i,** as in m**i**x.

► Sometimes the /ĕ/ sound is spelled in a different way. In the starred words *head* and *friend*, the /ĕ/ sound is spelled *ea* and *ie*.

Write each Spelling Word under its vowel sound.

Spelling Words

1. mix
2. milk
3. smell
4. last
5. head*
6. friend*
7. class
8. left
9. thick
10. send
11. thin
12. stick

/ă/ Sound

_____

_____

/ĭ/ Sound

_____

_____

/ĕ/ Sound

_____

_____

_____

_____

Name _____

Spelling Spree

Spelling Words

1. mix
2. milk
3. smell
4. last
5. head*
6. friend*
7. class
8. left
9. thick
10. send
11. thin
12. stick

Silly Rhymes Write a Spelling Word to complete each silly sentence. Each answer rhymes with the underlined word.

1. Will chewing gum _____ to a brick?
2. Don't pile bread on your _____!
3. Never drink _____ while wearing silk.
4. You have to be _____ to squeeze under a bin.
5. Fix the ladder and _____ the batter.
6. How can you tell if bees can _____?

1. _____   4. _____

2. _____   5. _____

3. _____   6. _____

Letter Math Write a Spelling Word by adding and taking away letters from the words below.

Example: d + fish - f = *dish*

7. spend - p   = _____

8. c + glass - g   = _____

9. leg - g + ft   = _____

10. fri + mend - m   = _____

11. blast - b   = _____

12. th + sick - s   = _____

Name _____

Proofreading and Writing

Proofreading Circle the five misspelled Spelling Words in the sign. Then write each word correctly.

> ### MY HAT IS LOST!
> Please help me find my hat. I don't know where I leaft it. The hat is green and has a thine blue ribbon. It is soft and kind of rumpled. The last time I had it was before clas on Monday. If you find it, please stik a note on my locker.
>
> A freind and classmate

Spelling Words

1. mix
2. milk
3. smell
4. last
5. head*
6. friend*
7. class
8. left
9. thick
10. send
11. thin
12. stick

1. _____

2. _____

3. _____

4. _____

5. _____

Write a Description Have you ever lost something that you liked very much, such as a piece of clothing or a toy?

On a separate sheet of paper, write a short description of the item you lost. Make sure to include details that would help someone recognize it. Use Spelling Words from the list.

Name _____

Find the Right Order

The words in the Lost Bin have simply been tossed in any old order. Put the words in alphabetical order and write them in the Found Bin.

LOST BIN

muddle	principal
paddle	suggest
squeeze	crazy
plunge	mutter
middle	groan

FOUND BIN

1. _____   6. _____

2. _____   7. _____

3. _____   8. _____

4. _____   9. _____

5. _____   10. _____

Finding Sentences

Name _____

Read each group of words. Write *sentence* if the words are a complete sentence. Write *fragment* if the words are not a complete sentence. Then rewrite each fragment as a complete sentence. Add a word or words from the box at the bottom of the page.

1. Floyd wanted a hat. _____

   _____

2. Examined a suit of armor. _____

   _____

3. The rumpled lucky hat. _____

   _____

4. Mona looked for her missing hat. _____

   _____

5. Floated on the water. _____

   _____

6. Flipped a coin. _____

   _____

Word Bank

adventures	disappeared	Floyd
Mona	the boat	Wendell
worked		

Name _____

Changing Fragments to Sentences

Use each fragment below in a complete sentence.

1. Floyd and his friend Wendell

_____

2. into a lost and found box

_____

3. loses her lucky hat

_____

4. looks like a dragon

_____

5. in the hat room

_____

6. an exciting adventure in a strange world

_____

7. decides which cave to explore

_____

8. a burgundy fez with a small gold tassel

_____

Name _____

Finding Sentences

Effective writers use complete sentences. Correct each sentence fragment. Write your revised sentence on each line. If it is a complete sentence, write the word *correct*.

Lucky Hats for Lucky Cats

1. Mona's cat. Likes Mona's lucky hat.

   _____

2. Laughs at the ridiculous cat.

   _____

3. The playful cat. Bites the floppy hat.

   _____

4. Then the cat runs away with the hat.

   _____

5. Chases her cat into the basement.

   _____

6. She hears. A meow.

   _____

7. Mona opens the suitcase.

   _____

8. The cat. Is on her lucky hat.

   _____

Name _____

Writing a Friendly Letter

The person I will write to: _____

My address: _____

_____

The date: _____

How I will greet the receiver: _____

Why I want to write: _____

_____

The most important thing I want to say: _____

_____

_____

Important details I want to include: _____

_____

_____

How I will close: _____

_____

Name _____

Using Commas in Dates and Places

▶ When writing dates, use a comma between the day and the year. **Example:** May 12, 2003

▶ Use a comma after the year except at the end of a sentence.

  Example: On June 30, 2003, my sister will be ten years old.

▶ Use a comma between a town or city and the state.

  Example: New Orleans, Louisiana

▶ Use a comma after the state except at the end of a sentence.

  Example: My brother goes to college in New Orleans, Louisiana, and we will visit him next month.

Proofread the letter and add commas where necessary.

653 Cauterskill Road
Catskills New York 12414
February 25 2005

Dear Uncle Frank,

Our class is taking a field trip to New York City. Mom and Dad are going to be parent helpers. We want to spend an evening with you. We take a bus to New York New York on May 12 2005 and return on the morning of May 14 2005. Can you let us know right away which date is best for you?

Your nephew,
Michael

Revising Your Personal Narrative

**Reread your story. What do you need to make it better?
Use this page to help you decide. Put a checkmark in the
box for each sentence that describes your personal narrative.**

Rings the Bell!

☐ The beginning catches the reader's interest.

☐ The story is told in sequence and is easy to follow.

☐ Everything in my story is important to the topic.

☐ The sentences flow smoothly and don't repeat unnecessary information.

☐ There are almost no mistakes.

Getting Stronger

☐ The beginning could be more interesting.

☐ The sequence of events isn't always clear.

☐ There are some things that don't relate to the topic.

☐ I could combine some sentences to make this flow better.

☐ There are a few mistakes.

Try Harder

☐ The beginning is boring.

☐ Events are out of order and confusing to the reader.

☐ The story doesn't relate to the main topic.

☐ There are a lot of mistakes.

Combining Sentences

**Combine each pair of sentences into one. Include all the
important parts of both sentences. Avoid repeating words.**

1. The water was cold. The water was full of sharks.

   _____

   _____

2. Nina dove in the water. Brenda dove in the water.

   _____

   _____

3. Paul screamed. Winston screamed.

   _____

4. Nina laughed. Nina shouted, "Come on in, fellas!"

   _____

   _____

5. Paul said, "No way!" Winston said, "No way!"

   _____

   _____

6. Brenda yelled, "These sharks are only toys!" Tina yelled,
   "These sharks are only toys!"

   _____

   _____

Name _____

Spelling Words

Look for spelling patterns you have learned to help you remember the Spelling Words on this page. Think about the parts that you find hard to spell.

Write the missing letters and apostrophe in the Spelling Words below.

1. hav _____

2. hav _____ _____ _____

3. f _____ _____ nd

4. ar _____ _____ nd

5. _____ ne

6. th _____ n

7. th _____ n

8. th _____ m

9. befo _____ _____

10. bec _____ _____ _____ e

11. _____ ther

12. _____ _____ ther

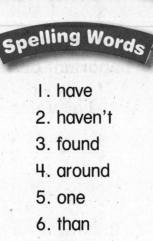
Study List On another sheet of paper, write each Spelling Word. Check the list to be sure you spell each word correctly.

Name _____

Spelling Spree

Sentence Fillers Write the Spelling Word from the list on this page that best completes each sentence.

1–2. "Scott, _____ you seen my coat?"

"No, I _____."

3. We drove _____ the block three times.

4. Our neighbors asked us to lend _____ our lawnmower.

5. For a while it was noisy, but _____ it got quiet.

6. We met at the theater _____ the movie started.

7. I don't want this one, I want the _____ one.

8. Tania _____ a five-dollar bill lying on the ground.

1. _____	5. _____
2. _____	6. _____
3. _____	7. _____
4. _____	8. _____

Spelling Words

1. have
2. haven't
3. found
4. around
5. one
6. than
7. then
8. them
9. before
10. because
11. other
12. mother

Word Clues Write the Spelling Word that fits each clue best.

9. You can use this word when you give a reason.

10. This word isn't a father, but a _____.

11. This word is the first thing you say when you count.

12. You can use this word when you compare two things.

9. _____	11. _____
10. _____	12. _____

Theme 1: **Off to Adventure!** 21

Name _____

Proofreading and Writing

Proofreading Circle the four misspelled Spelling Words in this postcard. Then write each word correctly on the lines below.

1. have
2. haven't
3. found
4. around
5. one
6. than
7. then
8. them
9. before
10. because
11. other
12. mother

Dear Peter,

    I just wanted to send a card to say hi befor I get going again. I fond this one in a little store in Yellowknife. Things are going great, and I'll have a lot of stories to tell when I get home. I'm sorry I havn't written in so long. I'll try to be better about it than I have been. Say hi to Mom and Dad, and tell then I'll call soon.

      Love,
      Kim

1. _____ 3. _____

2. _____ 4. _____

Adventure Dialogue Get together with another student and write a dialogue about an adventure. Both people in the dialogue can be off adventuring, or you can have one of them stay at home. Use Spelling Words from the list.

Name _____

Crossword Challenge!

Write the word that matches each clue in the puzzle.
Use the words in the box and your glossary for help.

Vocabulary

armor   comrades   endured   farewell
triumphant   troops   victorious

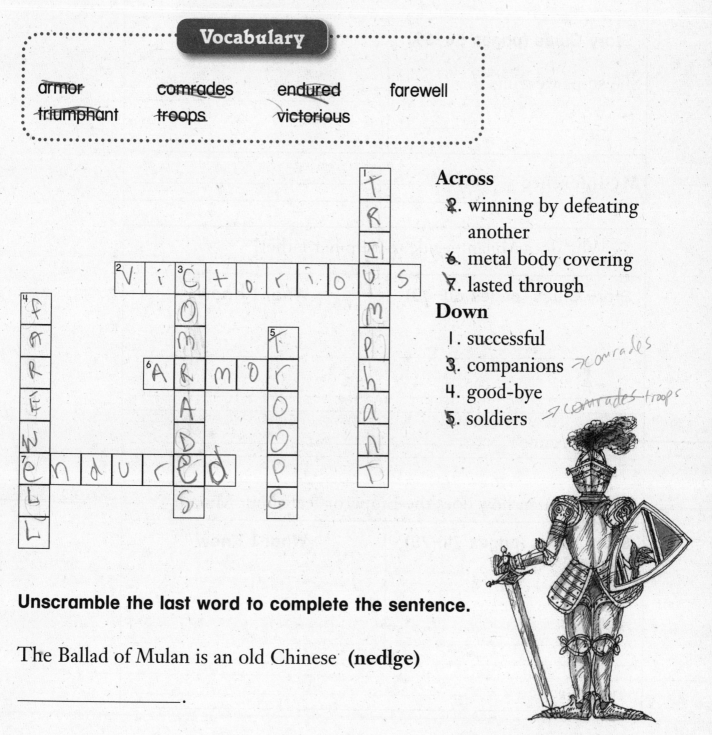

Across
2. winning by defeating another
6. metal body covering
7. lasted through

Down
1. successful
3. companions → comrades
4. good-bye
5. soldiers → comrades troops

Unscramble the last word to complete the sentence.

The Ballad of Mulan is an old Chinese **(nedlge)**

_____.

Name _____

Inference Chart

---

1. At the beginning of the story, how does Mulan feel?

Story Clues (pages 58–59)	What I Know
She stops weaving. _____	_____ _____

My Inference _____

---

2. Why does Mulan decide to help her father?

Story Clues (pages 60–63)	What I Know
because he is to old to fight	_____ _____

My Inference _____

---

3. Years later, how does the Emperor feel about Mulan?

Story Clues (pages 74–75)	What I Know
good _____ _____	_____ _____

My Inference _____

---

24   Theme 1: **Off to Adventure!**

Name _____

Answers About Mulan

Answer these questions about *The Ballad of Mulan*.

1. Why does the Emperor need troops?

to help fight in war

2. Why does Mulan go to war in her father's place?

3. After the war, why does the Emperor want to honor Mulan?

4. How does Mulan's family feel about having her come home?

5. When Mulan returns home, what does she choose to do?

6. What is the meaning of Mulan's statement about the rabbits?

7. Why do the Chinese still honor Mulan?

Make a Good Guess

**Read the story below. Then answer the
questions on the following page.**

The Ice Girl

Trolls were raiding the valley. They swooped down
from icy mountain caves, looking for workers and burning
houses and barns. Those unlucky enough to be caught
never saw daylight again. The people in the valley called a
meeting to deal with the problem.

Greta sat and knitted. Ever since Father had
fallen, Brother was doing all the family chores. Even at
this late hour, he had gone to town while Father slept.
Greta helped as best she could. In her spare time, she
knitted and knitted. Perhaps her work would help to
keep them from selling a cow.

Suddenly, Greta heard a noise outside. Trolls!
She slipped out a side door and stood waiting. Sure
enough, four ugly trolls peered around the barn. Greta stood
still. Slowly the trolls crept closer and closer, but Greta never
moved. Finally she felt the steam from their mouths. Then
she gathered all her strength and yelled, "Boo!" as loud as she
could. The trolls jumped. Then they ran off, as fast as their
feet could move. From that day on, no troll ever came back to
the valley again.

And to this day, people remember her deed. They have
even put up a sign. It reads, "Here is where Greta, the Ice
Girl, once lived. She drove the trolls away by saying '*Boo!*'"

Name _____

Make a Good Guess continued

Use clues from the story and what you know to answer each question below.

1. What did the people want to do about the trolls?

   _____

   _____

2. What happened to people who were caught by the trolls?

   _____

   _____

3. Why did Brother have to do all the family chores?

   _____

   _____

4. Why did Greta spend so much time knitting?

   _____

   _____

5. At the end, why were no trolls ever seen in the valley again?

   _____

   _____

Name _____

Syllabication

If you come across a word you can't pronounce, try dividing the
word into **syllables**, or parts of a word that are said out loud
as single sounds. Each word below has two syllables.
Each can be divided in a different way.

Divide the compound word into two words:

sunrise = sun • rise

**Divide the word between
two consonants:**

village = vil • lage

**Write the words below with spaces between the two
syllables. Divide them either between the words in a
compound word or between two consonants.**

1. mirror _____

_____

2. nightfall _____

_____

3. poster _____

_____

4. mountain _____

_____

5. downtown _____

_____

Name _____

More Short Vowels

A short vowel sound is usually spelled with one vowel followed by a consonant sound.

The /ŏ/ sound is usually spelled o, as in lot.

The /ŭ/ sound is usually spelled u, as in rub.

► Sometimes the /ŭ/ sound is spelled in a different way. In the starred words *does* and *won*, the /ŭ/ sound is spelled *oe* and *o*.

Write each Spelling Word under its vowel sound.

/ŏ/ Sound

_____

_____

_____

_____

_____

/ŭ/ Sound

_____

_____

_____

_____

_____

_____

Name _____

Spelling Spree

Finding Words Write the Spelling Word hidden in each of these words.

1. shutter   _____

2. wonderful   _____

3. plot   _____

4. rubber   _____

5. doesn't   _____

6. eardrum   _____

Spelling Words

1. pond
2. luck
3. drop
4. lot
5. rub
6. does*
7. drum
8. sock
9. hunt
10. crop
11. shut
12. won*

Questions Write a Spelling Word to answer each question.

7. What do you wear inside a shoe?

8. What does a farmer grow?

9. What can help you win a game?

10. What body of water is smaller than a lake?

11. What do lions do to get their dinner?

12. What do you call a tiny bead of water?

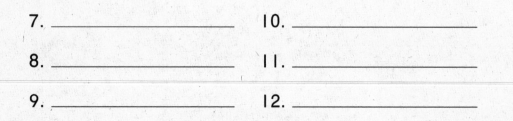

7. _____   10. _____

8. _____   11. _____

9. _____   12. _____

Name _____

Proofreading and Writing

Proofreading **Circle the five misspelled Spelling Words below. Then write each word correctly.**

The Emperor Praises Mulan

The Emperor welcomed General Mulan to the High Palace today. First, a soldier played a huge drume. Then the Emperor gave a speech. He told how Mulan was willing to droppe everything to join the army. He said the famous general did not win battles by luk, but by skill and bravery. Now, thanks to Mulan, the war is wone. No longer dose an invading army threaten China. The gates of the Great Wall are safely shut.

Spelling Words

1. pond
2. luck
3. drop
4. lot
5. rub
6. does*
7. drum
8. sock
9. hunt
10. crop
11. shut
12. won*

1. _____   4. _____

2. _____   5. _____

3. _____

Write a Story Long ago, in a land far away, a brave young girl named Mulan began a dangerous adventure. How would you begin an adventure story? What setting would you use? It could be a dark jungle or a distant planet, or it might be your own neighborhood.

On a separate sheet of paper, write the opening paragraph of an adventure story. Use Spelling Words from the list.

Name _____

Multiple Meaning Words

> **long** *adjective* **1.** Having great length: *a long river.*
> **2.** Lasting for a large amount of time: *a long movie.*
> **3.** Lasting a certain length: *The show was an hour long.*
> ◆ *adverb* Far away in the past: *The dinosaurs lived long ago.*
> ◆ *verb* To wish or want very much: *The children longed for an ice cream cone.*

For each of the following sentences, choose the correct definition of the underlined word. Write the definition on the line.

1. Long ago, a girl named Mulan went into battle.

    _____

2. A long line of soldiers crossed the mountain.

    _____

3. The town longed for peace to return.

    _____

4. It was a long way to the Yellow River.

    _____

5. Mulan longed to hear her mother's voice.

    _____

6. The war was ten years long.

    _____

Name _____

Classifying Sentences

Read and classify each sentence. Write *statement*, *question*, *command*, or *exclamation* on the line provided.

1. Why did Mulan fight in the army? _____

2. What an amazing girl she is! _____

3. Tell me what her journey was like. _____

4. She was surrounded by many dangers. _____

5. Mulan's family and friends were very proud of her.

_____

6. There she goes now! _____

7. Watch the victory parade. _____

8. Can you see Mulan at the front of the troops?

_____

9. The musicians sing a song about Mulan's

adventures. _____

10. How beautiful the music sounds!

_____

Name _____

Arranging Sentences

Arrange these sentences to create an interview with Mulan.
Four of the sentences are questions and four are the
answers to these questions. On the lines below, write each
question followed by its answer. Add the correct end marks.

I dressed in armor

Were you afraid

My father was too ill to fight

Are you glad to be home

I was terrified at first

Why did you join the army

Look at my face and see how
    happy I am

What did you wear

1. **Q:** _____

   A: _____

2. **Q:** _____

   A: _____

3. **Q:** _____

   A: _____

4. **Q:** _____

   A: _____

Name _____

Capitalizing and Punctuating Sentences

Capital letters and punctuation help us to understand writing.
Three students decided to act out a scene from *The Ballad
of Mulan.* Here is the script they wrote for the scene.
Check the capitalization and punctuation of each sentence.
Then rewrite the script, using the correct capitalization
and punctuation.

Soldier 1: Mulan, is that really you

1. _____

Soldier 2: how is this possible

2. _____

Soldier 1: are you really a girl

3. _____

Mulan: yes, I am you have not seen the real me

4. _____

Soldier 1: you are brave and amazing

5. _____

Soldier 2: what a remarkable girl you are

6. _____

Mulan: I had to save my father would you have let me fight
if I had dressed as a woman

7. _____

_____

Response Journal

Writing a Response Journal Entry Write about a story you
are reading now. Answer the questions. Use your own ideas.

Title of Story _____

How do I feel about what happens in the story?

_____

_____

How do I feel about the main character?

_____

_____

What do I think will happen next in the story?

_____

_____

What puzzles me about the story?

_____

_____

Which character in the story is most like me? Why?

_____

_____

Name _____

Capitalizing Days and Months

▶ Begin an entry in your journal with the day or date.
▶ Begin the name of the day of the week with a capital letter.

     Monday   Tuesday   Wednesday   Thursday
     Friday   Saturday   Sunday

▶ Begin the months of the year with capital letters.

     April 12
     November 24

Write each day or date correctly.

1. wednesday   _____

2. friday, november 18   _____

3. saturday   _____

4. monday, january 7   _____

5. thursday   _____

6. tuesday, may 8   _____

7. sunday   _____

Name _____

Adventure Advertisement

**Help rewrite this ad to make it more exciting.
Replace the words in parentheses with words from
the box. Fill in the blanks with the correct words.**

Visit Adventure _____ (Valley)! Ride

a canoe through _____ (fast, tiny

waterfalls in a river). Dock your canoe and cross the

river by stepping on huge _____

(round rocks). Walk past Silver Waterfall, where the

river looks like a boiling _____ (kettle).

After you've _____ (searched out) a

path, hike to the top of the waterfall. Be careful! To

climb the _____ (very steep) rock

walls, you'll have to find _____ (rock

shelves) on the sides of the cliffs.

**Answer the following question. (Hint: If you need
help, look at pages 92–93 in your textbook.)**

What is a waterfall?

_____

_____

Name _____

Cause and Effect Chart

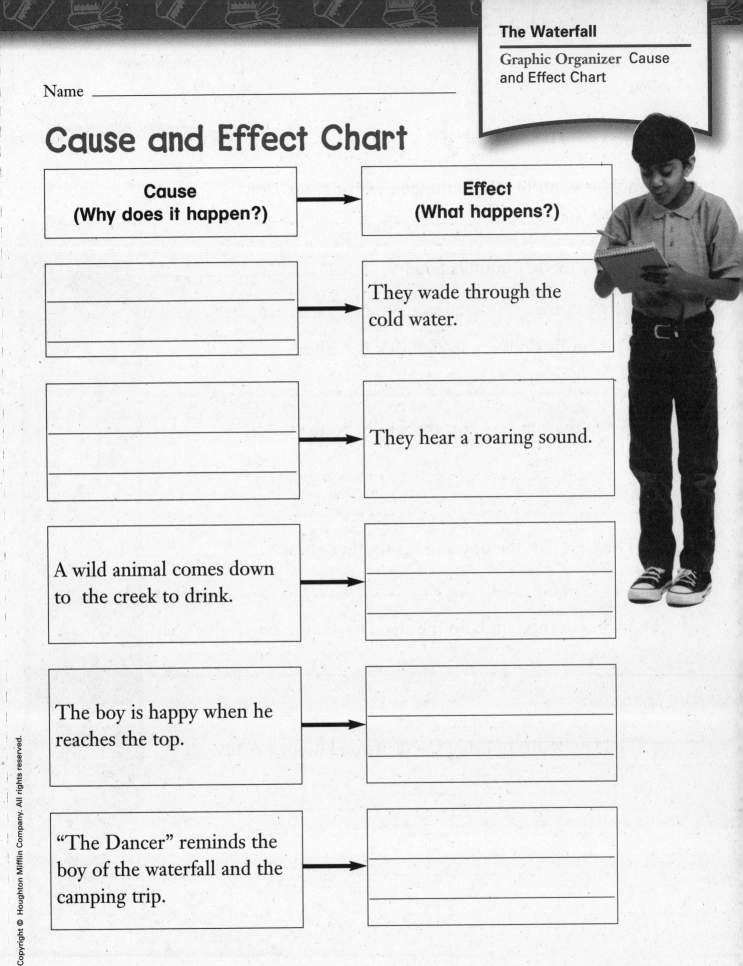

Cause (Why does it happen?)	Effect (What happens?)
_____ _____ _____	They wade through the cold water.
_____ _____ _____	They hear a roaring sound.
A wild animal comes down to the creek to drink.	_____ _____
The boy is happy when he reaches the top.	_____ _____
"The Dancer" reminds the boy of the waterfall and the camping trip.	_____ _____

Theme 1: **Off to Adventure!**   39

Name _____

Finish the Story

Complete each of the sentences with details from
The Waterfall.

1. In July the boy and his family _____

_____

2. The family finds a waterfall that is higher _____

_____

3. When the sun gets hot, the family keeps cool by

_____

_____

4. The next day, the boy and his brother climb _____

_____

5. As his parents climb up the steep rocks, the boy feels

_____

_____

6. The boy wants to bring the driftwood home because

_____

_____

Name _____

Causes and Effects

**Read the story. Think about what happens and why.
Then complete the chart on the next page.**

The Tornado

A rooster crowed, waking Lucy Sunders from a deep sleep.
She usually popped out of bed like buttons pop off a shirt, but
today she was tired. She had stayed up late last night reading.

Lucy looked out her window. The sky was a funny yellow-
gray, and there were no sounds. Then, across the fields, Lucy
saw a whirling dust cloud. It grew bigger and bigger. A
tornado was coming!

Lucy raced down the stairs, shouting, "Mama, Mama —
a tornado!"

Mrs. Sunders checked the sky. Then she grabbed the baby
from his swing. "Run! Run to the root cellar!" she shouted.

Lucy and her mother ran through the yard, and Lucy
pulled open the cellar door. She hurried down the steps. Her
mother locked the door and followed her into the darkness.

Quickly Mrs. Sunders lit the old lamp, and the light
glowed warmly. Lucy sighed. They were safe now.
Everything would be all right.

Name _____

Causes and Effects continued

In each box, write a cause or an effect from the story.

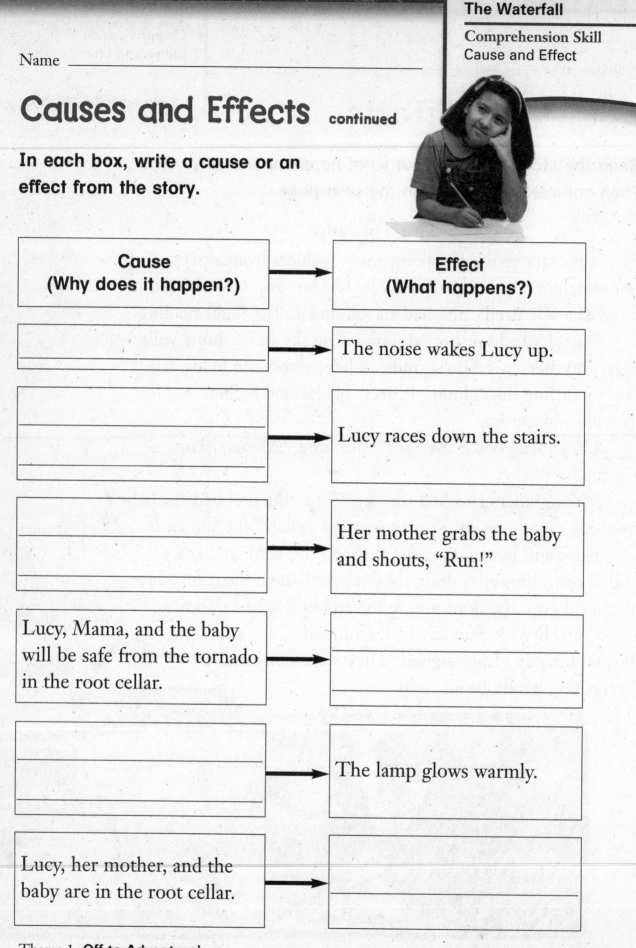

Cause (Why does it happen?)	Effect (What happens?)
	The noise wakes Lucy up.
	Lucy races down the stairs.
	Her mother grabs the baby and shouts, "Run!"
Lucy, Mama, and the baby will be safe from the tornado in the root cellar.	
	The lamp glows warmly.
Lucy, her mother, and the baby are in the root cellar.	

Name _____

Add the Ending

► For words that end with a vowel and a single
consonant, double the consonant before adding
-ed or *-ing*.

grip + p + ed = gripped   swim + m + ing = swimming

**Read the clues for the puzzle. For each one, choose
a word from the box with the same meaning as the
word in dark type. Complete the puzzle by adding
-ed or *-ing* to the word from the box.**

Word Bank

sip
drag
trap
drop
swim
dig
rip

Across

4. My brother and I **pulled**
the heavy branches.
5. The mountain lion **tore**
open the tent.
6. The raccoon **drank** water
from the stream.
7. The boys are **moving** in
the cold, clear water.

Down

1. My foot was **caught**
between two rocks!
2. Can you hear the water
falling?
3. The bear is **searching**
under the log for grubs.

Theme 1: **Off to Adventure!**   43

Name _____

The Vowel-Consonant-*e* Pattern

The long *a, i, o,* and *u* sounds are shown as /ā/, /ī/, /ō/, and /o͞o/. When you hear these sounds, remember that they are often spelled with the vowel-consonant-*e* pattern.

/ā/ s**a**v**e**   /ī/ l**i**f**e**   /ō/ sm**o**k**e**   /o͞o/ h**u**g**e**

► In the starred words *come* and *love,* the *o*-consonant-*e* pattern spells the /ŭ/ sound.

Write each Spelling Word under its vowel sound.

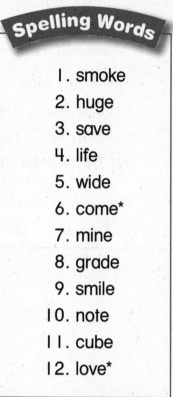

1. smoke
2. huge
3. save
4. life
5. wide
6. come*
7. mine
8. grade
9. smile
10. note
11. cube
12. love*

/ā/ or /ī/ Sound

_____

_____

_____

_____

/ō/ or /o͞o/ Sound

_____

_____

_____

No long vowel Sound

_____

_____

Name _____

Spelling Spree

Book Titles Write the Spelling Word that best
completes each book title. Remember to use capital
letters.

1. Sing Every _____ by B. A. Soprano

2. I _____ My Cats and Dogs by

   Ima Petowner

3. Dinosaurs Were _____! by Sy N. Tific

4. Live Your _____ to the Fullest by

   Hy Lee Adventurous

5. _____ to My Party by U. R. Invited

1. smoke
2. huge
3. save
4. life
5. wide
6. come*
7. mine
8. grade
9. smile
10. note
11. cube
12. love*

Puzzle Play Write a Spelling Word for each clue.
Then write the circled letters in order to spell
something you might see over a waterfall.

6. a year of school ___ ◯ ___ ___ ___

7. to keep for a while ___ ◯ ___ ___

8. a happy expression ___ ___ ◯ ___ ___

9. belongs to me ___ ___ ◯ ___

10. one shape for ice ___ ___ ◯ ___

11. fire can cause it ___ ___ ◯ ___

12. opposite of narrow ◯ ___ ___ ___

_____

Name _____

Proofreading and Writing

Proofreading Circle the five misspelled Spelling Words in the following notice. Then write each word correctly.

1. smoke
2. huge
3. save
4. life
5. wide
6. come*
7. mine
8. grade
9. smile
10. note
11. cube
12. love*

Attention All Visitors

Our wilderness areas are home to many kinds of animal and plant lif. They provide nesting areas for huje numbers of birds. People com from cities and towns all over the world to camp and hike in the wilderness. Show your respect and luv for the natural world. The children of the future must have the chance to enjoy these wid open spaces too.

1. _____   4. _____

2. _____   5. _____

3. _____

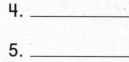

Write a Journal Entry Think about a special time you had outdoors. Where were you? Was it a field trip? A family outing? Or maybe a block party?

On a separate sheet of paper, describe where you were and what was special about the experience. Use Spelling Words from the list.

Name _____

Entry Words

Suppose the boy wrote this letter. Decide whether each underlined word would be an entry word in a dictionary or part of an entry. Write the word in the correct column.

Dear Malcolm,

     Our <u>camping</u> trip was great! We <u>backpacked</u> across a creek and set up our tents near the water. Then we had a <u>cookout</u> and watched the stars. We heard <u>growling</u> outside our tent, and I was scared. The next morning, we found tracks outside our tent. Dad said it was a <u>mountain lion</u>! The best part of the trip was when we <u>climbed</u> to the top of a huge waterfall. My <u>brother</u> and I were really proud, especially when Mom and Dad made it to the top! You'll have to see the great <u>souvenir</u> I brought back with me the next time you visit.

                  Your friend

Entry Word	Part of an Entry
_____	_____
_____	_____
_____	_____
_____	_____

Name _____

Connecting Subjects and Predicates

Read the sentence parts. Write S next to each subject. Write P next to each predicate. Then put the parts together to write six sentences. Write your sentences on the lines below.

a distant owl ___	block our path ___
the pounding water ___	crashes against the rocky
carries her own backpack ___	canyon ___
my father ___	puts on his hiking boots ___
the squirrels and	a few giant boulders ___
chipmunks ___	my sister ___
hoots to the moon ___	collect food on the ground ___

1. _____

2. _____

3. _____

4. _____

5. _____

6. _____

Name _____

Combining Subjects and Predicates

Combine each pair of sentences. Then write the new sentence on the line.

1. The sun shines. The sun heats the air.

   _____

2. My brother sees some animals. I see some animals.

   _____

3. The foxes run away. The deer run away.

   _____

4. We follow the trail. We find a cave.

   _____

5. The cave is dark. The cave is large.

   _____

6. We find our flashlight. We turn it on.

   _____

7. Bats live in caves. Bears live in caves.

   _____

8. Mother reminds us to be safe. Father reminds us to be safe.

   _____

Name _____

Subjects and Predicates

Write the complete subject and the complete predicate of each of the following sentences in the correct column.

1. We went camping.
2. Our new tent is very light.
3. The sunset was beautiful.
4. A full moon glows.
5. My sister woke up at sunrise.
6. She cooked breakfast over the campfire.
7. Our entire family walked to the canyon.
8. The rocky canyon is full of dangerous places.
9. My father and I spotted the waterfall.
10. The rushing water splashed our faces.

Subjects

_____

_____

_____

_____

_____

_____

_____

_____

_____

_____

Predicates

_____

_____

_____

_____

_____

_____

_____

_____

_____

_____

Name _____

Reasons and Facts

**Use this page to plan your explanation. Then number
your reasons or facts in the order you will use them.**

Topic: _____

_____

_____

Topic Sentence: _____

_____

_____

Reason/Fact: _____	Reason/Fact: _____
_____	_____
_____	_____
Reason/Fact: _____	Reason/Fact: _____
_____	_____
_____	_____

Name _____

Improving Your Writing

► Sometimes questions can be changed into
statements by moving the words around.
Are the children's parents good climbers?
The children's parents are good climbers.

► Sometimes words must be added, removed,
or changed to make a question into a statement.
Did most readers like the story?
Most readers liked the story.

► Changing the question on a test into a statement can
help you write a good topic sentence and focus your ideas.
Why is climbing exciting?
There are several reason why climbing is exciting.

Change each question into a statement.

1. What are some of the family's favorite activities?

_____

2. Did everyone in the class like the action story?

_____

3. Who are the main characters in this story?

_____

_____

4. Why is swimming under a waterfall fun?

_____

5. What types of movies does their family like to see?

_____

Name _____

Choosing the Best Answer

Use the test-taking strategies and tips you have learned to help you answer these questions. You may go back to *The Waterfall* if you need to. This practice will help you when you take this kind of test.

Read each question. Fill in the circle next to the best answer.

1 Why did the family wade through the cold water?

○ They wanted to cool off in the heat of the summer.

○ The rocks along the creek were too slippery to climb.

○ They were looking for the waterfall.

○ There was poison oak along the banks of the creek.

2 What was the first clue the family had that a waterfall was nearby?

○ They heard a roaring sound.

○ They saw a rainbow in the sky.

○ They felt the mist spray on their faces.

○ They saw a steep rock slope.

3 Why did Dad say, "End of the road," when the family got to the waterfall?

○ The trail they were on ended at the waterfall.

○ He thought the waterfall was too dangerous to climb.

○ The waterfall was as far as he wanted the family to go.

○ Once they got to the waterfall, he was ready to go home.

Name _____

Choosing the Best Answer

continued

4   What happened that made the older boy feel scared before
    he fell asleep?

○ He heard something in the brush.

○ He thought about climbing the waterfall.

○ He saw a wild animal near the camp.

○ He thought the family was lost.

5   What made the tracks near the family's camp?

○ a deer

○ a grizzly bear

○ a wolf

○ a mountain lion

6   What did the family decide to do after finding the tracks?

○ go back the way they had come

○ return home

○ climb the waterfall

○ contact the park ranger

Name _____

Spelling Review

Write Spelling Words from the list to answer the questions.

1–17. Which seventeen words have short vowels?

1. _____   10. _____

2. _____   11. _____

3. _____   12. _____

4. _____   13. _____

5. _____   14. _____

6. _____   15. _____

7. _____   16. _____

8. _____   17. _____

9. _____

18–25. Which eight words have the
vowel-consonant-*e* pattern?

18. _____   22. _____

19. _____   23. _____

20. _____   24. _____

21. _____   25. _____

Spelling Words

1. drum
2. huge
3. last
4. drop
5. class
6. left
7. wide
8. mix
9. send
10. save
11. smell
12. stick
13. note
14. thick
15. hunt
16. thin
17. grade
18. lot
19. cube
20. pond
21. life
22. sock
23. luck
24. shut
25. smile

Name _____

Spelling Spree

Book Titles Write the Spelling Word that best completes each funny book title. Remember to use capital letters.

1. class
2. mix
3. send
4. smell
5. stick
6. pond
7. sock
8. drum
9. huge
10. grade
11. cube
12. smile

Example: *The Great _____ from Planet X*
by I. C. Starrs   <u>Escape</u>

1. *Put an Ice _____ in My Glass and Other Science Experiments* by Sy N. Seen

2. *A _____ Is a Frown Upside Down* by Mary Timz

3. *My First Day in _____ 3: A True Story* by Ima Newcomer

4. *The Mystery in the Third Grade _____* by Minnie Klooz

5. *_____ Us a Post Card* by U. R. A. Riter

6. *Do I _____ Cookies?* by I. M. Hungree

1. _____   4. _____

2. _____   5. _____

3. _____   6. _____

One, Two, Three! Write the Spelling Word that belongs in each group.

7. piano, guitar, _____   10. stir, blend, _____

8. big, large, _____   11. shirt, shoe, _____

9. lake, river, _____   12. twig, branch, _____

Name _____

Proofreading and Writing

Proofreading Circle the five misspelled Spelling Words below. Then write each word correctly.

January 12—Today I went on a treasure hunte. I spent a lott of time looking for the treasure in a thic grove of trees and near the pond. I didn't have any luk. Maybe somebody will drap a clue that I will find!

1. _____   4. _____

2. _____   5. _____

3. _____

A Newspaper Article **Write a Spelling Word that means the same as each underlined word or words.**

Jeremy is a 6. <u>skinny</u> boy in Mr. Boyd's third grade 7. <u>group</u>. All of his 8. <u>years of being</u> Jeremy had heard about a buried treasure. One day he found a 9. <u>short letter</u> in his attic. It was all that was 10. <u>still around</u> of his grandfather's things. He 11. <u>closed</u> the door and read. "Keep your eyes 12. <u>all the way</u> open," it said. "Look under the 13. <u>final</u> tree in the yard." There Jeremy found a journal that he will 14. <u>keep</u>.

6. _____ 9. _____ 12. _____

7. _____ 10. _____ 13. _____

8. _____ 11. _____ 14. _____

Write a Letter On a separate sheet of paper, write to a friend about a buried treasure you hope to find. Use the Spelling Review Words.

Spelling Words

1. lot
2. left
3. thick
4. life
5. thin
6. last
7. luck
8. note
9. class
10. hunt
11. drop
12. wide
13. save
14. shut

Theme 1: **Off to Adventure!**   57

Celebrating Traditions

Describe a tradition that you celebrate. When do you celebrate it? Who shares the celebration with you? What is your favorite part of this tradition?

○ _____
_____
_____
_____
_____
○ _____
_____

List any traditions you would like to learn about.

○ _____
_____
_____
_____
_____

Name _____

Celebrating Traditions

Fill in the chart as you read the stories.

The Keeping Quilt

What tradition is celebrated in this selection?

Why is this tradition important to those who celebrate it?

Anthony Reynoso: Born to Rope

What tradition is celebrated in this selection?

Why is this tradition important to those who celebrate it?

The Talking Cloth

What tradition is celebrated in this selection?

Why is this tradition important to those who celebrate it?

Dancing Rainbows

What tradition is celebrated in this selection?

Why is this tradition important to those who celebrate it?

Name _____

Quilt Crossword

Write the word that matches each clue in
the puzzle. Use the vocabulary words for help.

Vocabulary

border
gathering
needles
scraps
sewn
threaded

Across

4. edge

6. tools for sewing

Down

1. coming together

2. leftover pieces

3. passed through the eye
   of a needle

5. put together with a
   needle and thread

Name _____

Author's Family Chart

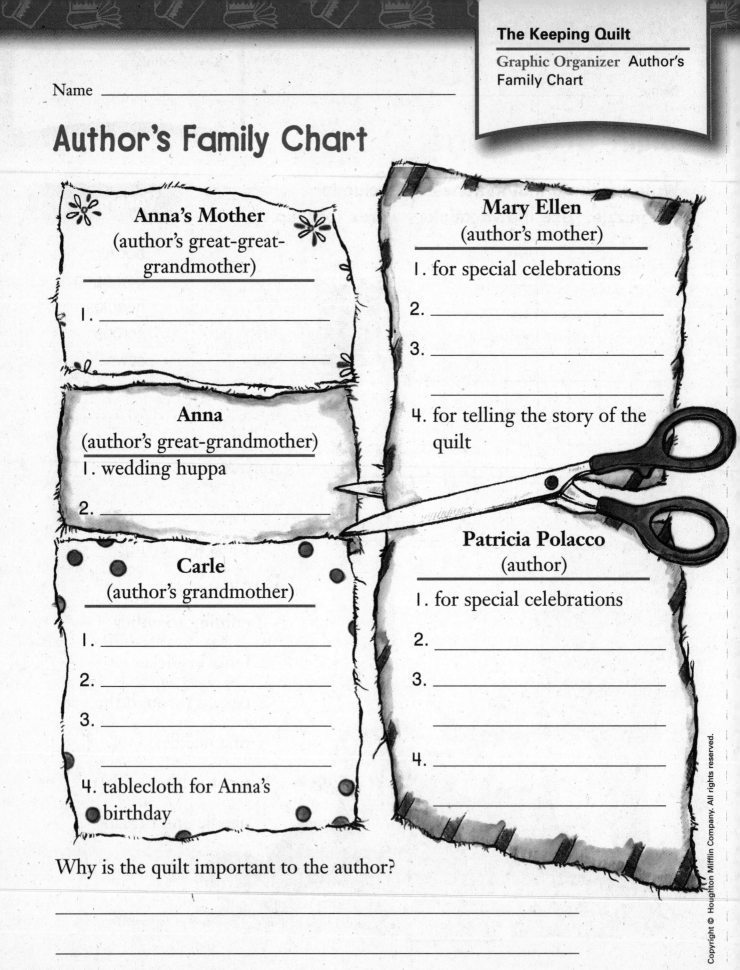

Anna's Mother
(author's great-great-
grandmother)
_____

1. _____

2. _____

Anna
(author's great-grandmother)
1. wedding huppa

2. _____

Carle
(author's grandmother)
_____

1. _____

2. _____

3. _____

_____

4. tablecloth for Anna's
   birthday

Mary Ellen
(author's mother)
_____

1. for special celebrations

2. _____

3. _____

_____

4. for telling the story of the
   quilt

Patricia Polacco
(author)
_____

1. for special celebrations

2. _____

3. _____

_____

4. _____

_____

Why is the quilt important to the author?

_____

_____

Name _____

Piece It Together

Finish each statement with details from *The Keeping Quilt*.

1. Anna's mother decides to make the quilt because

    _____

    _____

2. When Carle grows up, Great-Gramma Anna passes
   the quilt on to her. She

    _____

    _____

3. Over the years, people in the family use the quilt as

    _____

    _____

4. Mary Ellen tells her daughter (the author) whose

    _____

    _____

5. Mary Ellen also is lucky enough to tell the story of the quilt to

    _____

    _____

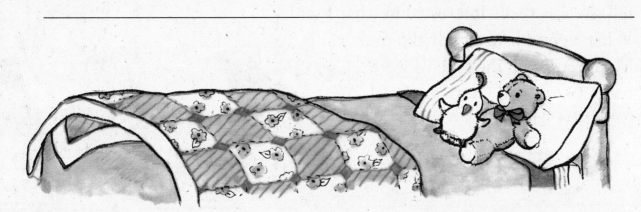

Name _____

An Author's View

Read the story. Then finish the chart on the next page.

Foxtails

When I first saw Grandma Sorensen in her doorway, she seemed ten feet tall and skinny! She frowned as she squinted into the sun and watched our car. Would I like her?

In the living room, Grandma Sorensen gave each of us a big hug. Then she and Mom began talking. Soon they were laughing about things Mom did as a girl. Once she fell out of their apple tree and broke her arm. Then Grandma told how she too had fallen out of an apple tree and broken her arm. That was when she was a girl in Denmark. I said, "I'm never going to climb apple trees!" Grandma laughed.

Later, after Mom had left for a meeting, Grandma suggested that we make my mother a treat, the one she loved best at my age. In the kitchen, Grandma let me mix flour, sugar, eggs, butter, and vanilla together to make a stiff dough. Then she showed me how to pinch off a small piece of dough, roll it, and twist it into a "foxtail." She didn't mind that I made the tails a bit crooked.

As we worked, Grandma asked me about school and what I wanted to be when I grew up. From her questions I could tell she was really interested in what I said. What a good listener! By the time Mom returned, the foxtails were ready to eat, and Grandma and I were best friends.

Name _____

An Author's View continued

Use story details to finish this chart. Tell how the author feels about her grandmother.

Scene	Details About Grandma	Author's Feelings About Grandma
The Doorway	1. _____ _____ 2. _____ _____	_____ _____ _____ _____
The Living Room	1. _____ _____ 2. _____	_____ _____ _____
The Kitchen	1. _____ _____ 2. _____	_____ _____ _____

If you met Grandma Sorensen, do you think you would like her? Why or why not? Use complete sentences.

_____

_____

_____

Name _____

Compound Mix-up

Write a compound word to match each picture clue.
Each word is made up of two words from the Word Bank.

Word Bank

dog	bug	pot	lady	flower	flag
fly	dragon	tooth	rain	fish	bow
house	brush	pole	moon	star	light

_____   _____   _____

_____   _____   _____

_____   _____   _____

Combine two words from the Word Bank to make a new compound word.

_____

Name _____

More Long Vowel Spellings

To spell a word with the /ā/ sound, remember that /ā/ can be spelled *ai* or *ay*. To spell a word with the /ē/ sound, remember that /ē/ can be spelled *ea* or *ee*.

| /ā/ | ai, ay | **pa**int, cl**ay** |
| /ē/ | ea, ee | l**ea**ve, f**ee**l |

► In the starred words *neighbor*, *eight*, and *weigh*, the /ā/ sound is spelled *eigh*.

Write each Spelling Word under its vowel sound.

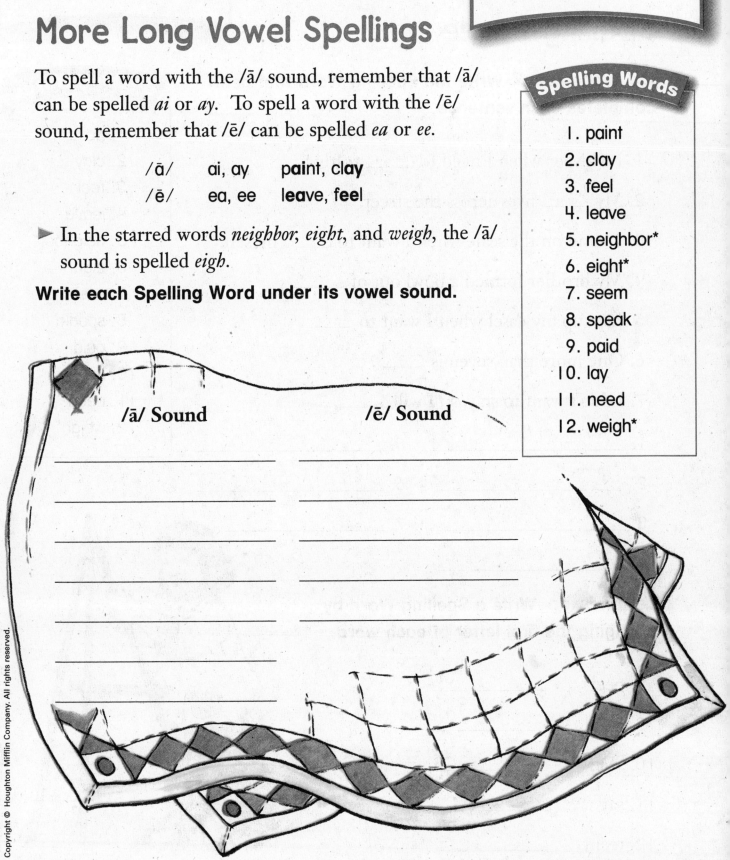

/ā/ Sound   **/ē/ Sound**

Name _____

Spelling Spree

Fill in the Blank Write the Spelling Word that best
completes each sentence.

1. I whisper when I need to _____ softly.

2. My _____ lives across the street.

3. I stand on the scale when I want to _____ myself.

4. My brother formed a bowl out of _____.

5. I set up my easel when I want to _____.

6. One more than seven is _____.

7. I don't want to stay, so I will _____.

1. _____   5. _____

2. _____   6. _____

3. _____   7. _____

4. _____

Letter Swap Write a Spelling Word by
changing the first letter of each word.

8. peel   _____

9. maid   _____

10. seed   _____

11. say   _____

12. teem   _____

Spelling Words

1. paint
2. clay
3. feel
4. leave
5. neighbor*
6. eight*
7. seem
8. speak
9. paid
10. lay
11. need
12. weigh*

Name _____

Proofreading and Writing

Proofreading Circle the five misspelled Spelling
Words in this invitation. Then write each word
correctly.

Dear New Neighbor,

    Please join me and some of the other tenants in
the building for a quilting party. I have enough
needles and thread for eaght helpers. You don't ned
to be a sewing expert. The work will seam easy, and
we will all get to know one another. Later we will
have tea and cake. The party will be in my
apartment next Monday evening. If you are
interested, spek to me soon. If you prefer, you can
leve a note in my mailbox instead.

          Sincerely,
          Natasha Pushkin

1. paint
2. clay
3. feel
4. leave
5. neighbor*
6. eight*
7. seem
8. speak
9. paid
10. lay
11. need
12. weigh*

1. _____   4. _____

2. _____   5. _____

3. _____

Write a Description If you were going to design a quilt
like the one in the story, what would it look like?

**On a separate sheet of paper, write about a quilt you would
design. Tell what material you would use and why. Use
Spelling Words from the list.**

Name _____

Word Family Reunion

Select the words that belong to the word family for "back."
Then arrange the words on the chart and define each one.
Check your work in a dictionary.

Word Bank

backward	bacteria	backyard	bachelor	backboard
backbone	backfire	background	backpack	backup

The Back Family

Word	Meaning
1. _____	_____
2. _____	_____
3. _____	_____
4. _____	_____
5. _____	_____
6. _____	_____
7. _____	_____
8. _____	_____

Name _____

In Search of Common Nouns

Circle the common noun or nouns in each group of words.

1. big   room

2. quilt   sewed   needle

3. house   talk   enjoy   people

4. blanket   warm   sister   friend

5. happy   silly   story   angry

6. curious   city   cheerful   sad

Write the circled nouns in the correct square below.

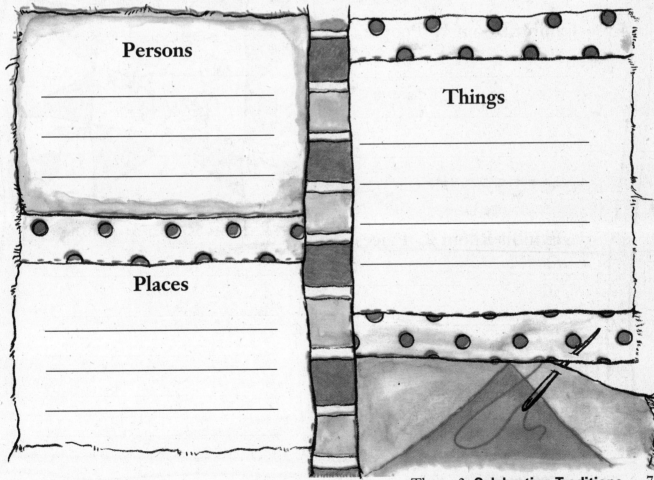

Persons

_____

_____

_____

Things

_____

_____

_____

_____

Places

_____

_____

_____

Name _____

Common Nouns in Signs

Find the common nouns in the report. Write each common noun in the correct exhibit room below.

A Visit to the Museum

My friends and I visited a museum. There we saw a collection of wonderful old quilts. Some of them were made by pioneers. Many of the blankets showed children, flowers, and trees. One showed all fifty states.

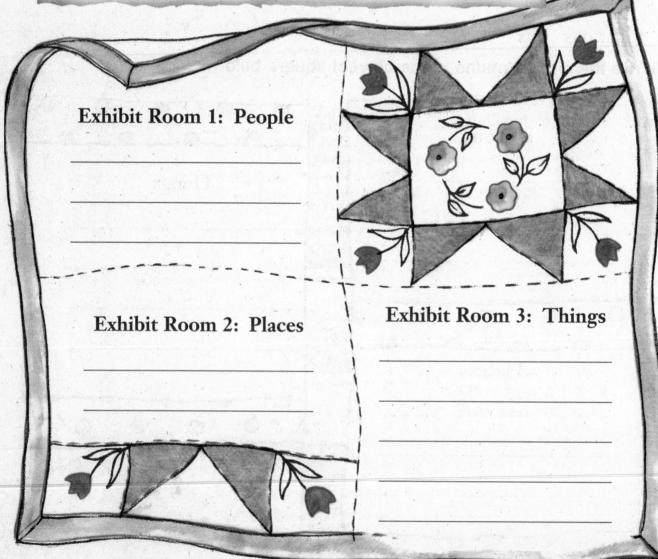

Exhibit Room 1: People

_____

_____

_____

Exhibit Room 2: Places

_____

_____

Exhibit Room 3: Things

_____

_____

_____

_____

Commas in a Series

Proofread each sentence. Add commas to separate each series of three or more words. Remove all unnecessary commas.

1. Our attic is filled with boxes bags and books.

   _____

2. I found my great-grandfather's hat gloves and cane.

   _____

3. The cane was carved with tigers lions and elephants.

   _____

4. I also found old journals photographs and drawings.

   _____

5. One photograph shows my aunt uncle and cousin.

   _____

6. My great-grandmother lived on a farm with chickens cows horses and pigs.

   _____

   _____

7. In her diary, she described her, friends relatives and visitors.

   _____

8. Her hopes wishes and dreams, bring every page to life.

   _____

Name _____

Paragraphs That Compare and Contrast

Use the chart on this page to help you plan paragraphs that compare and contrast. Write what the paragraphs will be about. Write two or three interesting details that show how the people, places, and things are alike. Then write how they are different. Use the details you record in your writing.

What I Will Compare and Contrast

_____

_____

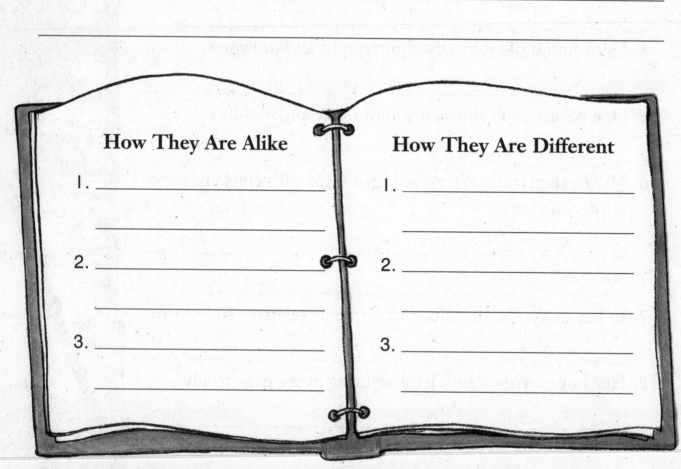

How They Are Alike

1. _____

   _____

2. _____

   _____

3. _____

   _____

How They Are Different

1. _____

   _____

2. _____

   _____

3. _____

   _____

Write your paragraphs that compare and contrast on a separate sheet of paper. Include the details you wrote above.

Name _____

Sentence Combining

► Connect two related sentences with a comma and
a joining word to make a compound sentence.

► Use a comma and the word *and* to create a
compound sentence that makes a comparison.

   Example: The gifts were part of the women's bouquets, **and**
   each gift was a symbol of something important for a good life.

► Use a comma and the word *but* to create a compound
sentence that makes a contrast.

   Example: At the first weddings, the women wore
   wedding dresses, **but** later some women wore suits.

**Write a compound sentence. Combine the sentences
with a comma and the joining word in parentheses ( ).**

1. The women loved the keeping quilt. They used it to keep
   their family's traditions alive. (and)

   _____

   _____

2. The women's weddings were alike in some ways. They were
   also different. (but)

   _____

   _____

3. The quilt was used as a cape. It was used as a huppa too. (and)

   _____

Theme 2: **Celebrating Traditions** 75

Name _____

Revising Your
Instructions

**Reread your instructions. What do you need to make them
better? Use this page to help you decide. Put a checkmark
in the box for each sentence that describes your instructions.**

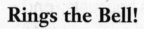

Rings the Bell!

☐ The goal of my instructions is clearly stated.

☐ The steps are clear and in the right sequence.

☐ The information that I presented is complete.
I included all the necessary details.

☐ I used exact words to make my directions as
precise as possible.

Getting Stronger

☐ I could make the goal of the instructions clearer.

☐ My steps aren't always clear. The sequence may need
work.

☐ I need to add some important information.

☐ I could add exact words to improve my instructions.

Try Harder

☐ The goal of my instructions is not stated.

☐ The steps aren't clear, and they are out of order.

☐ I left out some very important information.

☐ I need to use more exact words.

Name _____

Using Exact Nouns

Circle the letter of the noun that best replaces each underlined word or phrase.

1. Do you want to be a movie person who acts?

   a. lawyer   b. watcher   c. star   d. Venus

2. First, you need to have a good head of fuzzy stuff.

   a. hair   b. ears   c. smile   d. connections

3. Then, you need some cool clothes and a pair of dark eye things.

   a. pupils   b. carrots   c. cups   d. sunglasses

4. Next, you need a big, fancy house with a big thing of water.

   a. garage   b. door   c. pool   d. yard

5. You'll need to eat at all the best eating places.

   a. restaurants   b. stations   c. rinks   d. garages

6. Of course, you need to have an agent and a person who represents you legally.

   a. judge   b. sheriff   c. lawyer   d. partner

7. Do you need any actual acting stuff?

   a. manners   b. talent   c. rules   d. clothes

8. "It helps, but it's not a must," say all the top Hollywood movie leaders.

   a. sleepers   b. sellers   c. drivers   d. directors

Name _____

Spelling Words

Look for spelling patterns you have learned to help you remember the Spelling Words on this page. Think about the parts that you find hard to spell.

Write the missing letters and apostrophe in the Spelling Words below.

1. n ____ ____

2. o ____ ____

3. f ____ r

4. ____ ____ most

5. ____ ____ so

6. can ____ ____

7. ca ____ ____ ot

8. ab ____ ____ t

9. ____ ____ ways

10. ____ ____ day

11. unt ____ ____

12. ag ____ ____ n

Spelling Words

1. now
2. off
3. for
4. almost
5. also
6. can't
7. cannot
8. about
9. always
10. today
11. until
12. again

Study List On another sheet of paper, write each Spelling Word. Check the list to be sure you spell each word correctly.

Spelling Spree

Word Switch **For each sentence, write a Spelling Word to take the place of the underlined word or words.**

1. Let's go ride the roller coaster <u>another time</u>!
2. I'm in a real hurry, so I can't talk <u>at this time</u>.
3. Sofia <u>every time</u> has a box of raisins in her lunch.
4. My mom said that you can come to the beach <u>too</u>, if you want.
5. It's been <u>not quite</u> three years since we had a snowstorm.
6. They said on the radio that <u>the current day</u> is the first day of fall.

1. _____	4. _____
2. _____	5. _____
3. _____	6. _____

Letter Math **Add and subtract letters from the words below to make Spelling Words. Write the new words.**

7. foot – ot + r = _____

8. cart – rt + n't = _____

9. able – le + out = _____

10. order – rder + ff = _____

11. canned – ed + ot = _____

12. unit – it + til = _____

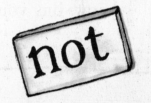

Spelling Words

1. now
2. off
3. for
4. almost
5. also
6. can't
7. cannot
8. about
9. always
10. today
11. until
12. again

Name _____

Proofreading and Writing

Proofreading Find and circle the four misspelled Spelling Words in this poster. Then write each word correctly.

Brazilian Festival

On June 15th, the annual Brazilian Festival will take place agin. There will be plenty of traditional music, dancing, and Brazilian food. Our festival is allways a good time. And if you miss this one, you won't get another chance until next year! Tickets are on sale know. Buy yours todday!

1. _____   3. _____

2. _____   4. _____

✏️ **Write a Poem** Think about a tradition that's important to you. It can be one shared by a lot of people, or one that just your family shares. Then write a poem about the tradition. Use Spelling Words from the list.

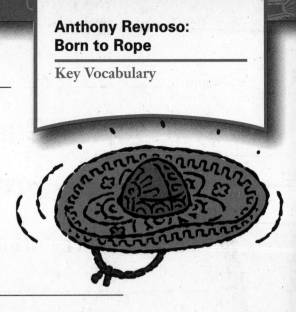

Name _____

Rodeo Words

**Label each sentence True or False. If the
sentence is false, rewrite it to make it correct.**

1. A rodeo is a sporting event for cowboys.

   _____

   _____

2. Ceremonies are a set of acts that honor an event.

   _____

   _____

3. A celebrity is a person who is not very well-known.

   _____

   _____

4. An exhibition is a public show or display.

   _____

   _____

5. Experts are people who are beginners at an activity.

   _____

   _____

6. Performers are people who watch a show.

   _____

   _____

Categories Chart

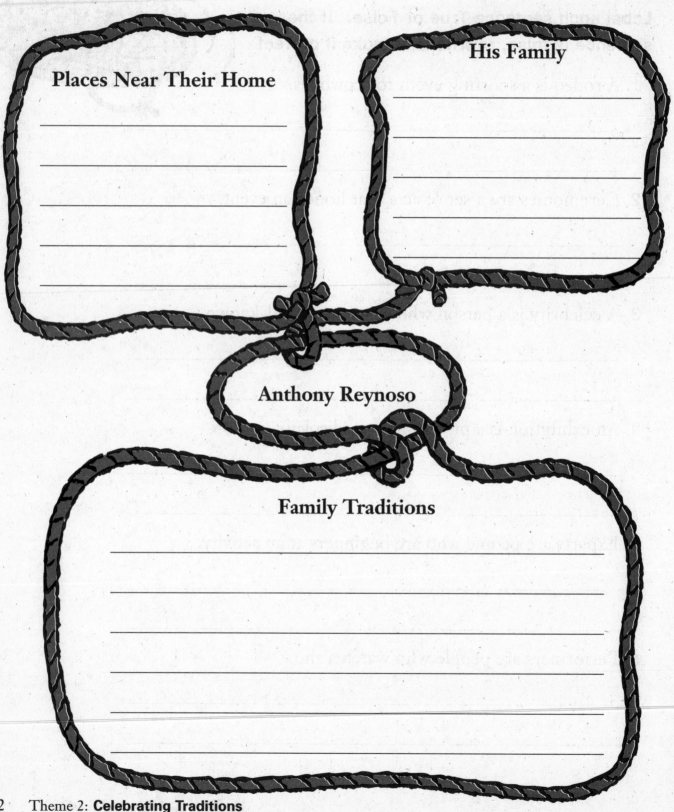

Places Near Their Home

_____
_____
_____
_____

His Family

_____
_____
_____

Anthony Reynoso

Family Traditions

_____
_____
_____
_____
_____

Name _____

Read All About It!

**Answer the reporter's questions as if you were
Anthony Reynoso. Use complete sentences.**

1. What do you, your father, and your grandfather do on your
   grandfather's ranch?

   _____

   _____

2. Why do you practice roping so much?

   _____

   _____

3. Where do you and your dad often go on Saturdays and
   what do you do there?

   _____

   _____

4. What else do you do in your spare time?

   _____

   _____

   _____

5. What special event are you looking forward to? Why?

   _____

   _____

   _____

Name _____

Family Categories

Read the story. Then complete the chart on the next page.

No Time to Spare

It's hard to find a good time to get in touch with my Aunt Mickey Sobol. It's even harder to reach my cousins Karen and Ike. That's because they're always busy.

Their day starts at sunup when Karen and Ike head for the barn to feed their sheep. Meanwhile, Aunt Mickey does chores and fixes the lunches. After breakfast, my cousins take the bus to school, and Aunt Mickey leaves for work.

Each day, Aunt Mickey walks a mile to the little store she runs by the lake. People from nearby vacation homes often stop there, so she's always busy.

After school, Karen and Ike head for the animal shelter down the road. Both of them want to be animal doctors, so they like to help with the animals.

After dinner and homework, the family relaxes. Ike usually reads, and Karen talks to a friend on the computer. Aunt Mickey enjoys weaving colorful blankets made of wool from their sheep.

Name _____

Family Categories

Write story details to complete this chart.

Family Members

_____

_____

_____

Places Near Their Home
their barn

_____

_____

_____

The Sobol
Family

Activities
going to school

_____

_____

_____

_____

Name _____

Perfect Plurals

► Add -*s* to form the plural of most nouns.
   hat/hat**s**

► Add -*es* to form the plural of nouns that end in *ch*.
   lunch/lunch**es**

► When a noun ends with a consonant and *y*,
   change the *y* to *i* and add -*es*.
   penny/penn**ies**

Word Bank

hobby
ranch
pony
family
rope
branch
blueberry
whale
hat
sandwich

**Write the plural of the word that matches each clue
in the puzzle. Use the Word Bank for help.**

Across

   2. parts of a tree
   5. small horses
   7. strong, thick cords
   8. lunch items
   9. very large sea animals

Down

   1. covers for the head
   2. small blue fruits
   3. activities done for fun
   4. groups of parents and their
      children
   6. large farms where cattle are
      raised

Name _____

The Long *o* Sound

To spell a word with the /ō/ sound, remember that this sound can be spelled *oa*, *ow*, or *o*.

/ō/   oa, ow, o   c**oa**ch, bl**ow**, h**o**ld

► In the starred words *sew* and *though*, the /ō/ sound is spelled *ew* and *ough*.

Write each Spelling Word under its spelling of the /ō/ sound.

oa Spelling

_____

_____

_____

ow Spelling

_____

_____

o Spelling

_____

_____

_____

Another Spelling

_____

_____

Spelling Words

1. coach
2. blow
3. float
4. hold
5. sew*
6. though*
7. sold
8. soap
9. row
10. own
11. both
12. most

Theme 2: **Celebrating Traditions**   87

Name _____

Spelling Spree

Word Maze Begin at the arrow and follow the Word Maze to find seven Spelling Words. Write the words in order.

eanblowfpthoughrwfloatvholdexrowbotheisold

Spelling Words

1. coach
2. blow
3. float
4. hold
5. sew*
6. though*
7. sold
8. soap
9. row
10. own
11. both
12. most

1. _____
2. _____
3. _____
4. _____
5. _____
6. _____
7. _____

Classifying Write the Spelling Word that belongs in each group of words.

8. have, possess, _____

9. mend, stitch, _____

10. teacher, trainer, _____

11. toothpaste, shampoo, _____

12. lots, many, _____

88 Theme 2: **Celebrating Traditions**

Name _____

Proofreading and Writing

Proofreading Circle the five misspelled Spelling
Words in this poster. Then write each word correctly.

Spelling Words

1. coach
2. blow
3. float
4. hold
5. sew*
6. though*
7. sold
8. soap
9. row
10. own
11. both
12. most

May 19, Sedona Fairgrounds
Roping Exhibition!

See bothe Reynoso roping champions!

Be ready to holed on to your hats! Thrill to the

tricks of Arizona's moast talented father and son

rope spinners. You won't believe your oun eyes!

Tickets will be soled at the gate.

1. _____   4. _____

2. _____   5. _____

3. _____

Write a Story About Yourself Have you ever worked hard to
learn something? Maybe it was learning to swim, ride a bike,
or even tie your shoes.
**On a separate sheet of paper, write about a time when you
worked very hard to learn something. Tell what the experience
was like. Use Spelling Words from the list.**

Name _____

Word Sort

Parts of a Dictionary Read each word. Then alphabetize
the words and place each word with the correct guide words.

snore	lentil	outing
outfit	outgoing	lent
lesson	snowdrift	outlet
snow	leopard	snout

lengthy/let

_____

_____

_____

snip/snowdrop

_____

_____

_____

outfielder/outnumber

_____

_____

_____

Name _____

Capital Letters

Capitalize each proper noun on the list below.

1. anthony reynoso _____

2. mexico _____

3. tuesday _____

4. fifth avenue _____

5. martha cooper _____

6. fourth of july _____

7. united states of america _____

8. *the keeping quilt* _____

9. mary ellen suarez _____

10. sedona, arizona _____

Write the proper noun or nouns in each sentence.

11. After school, Dad shows me a new rope trick. _____

12. On Saturday, we go to the Sedona Rodeo. _____

13. I read the new book by Ginger Gordon. _____

14. Her first book was *My Two Worlds*. _____

15. She is a teacher in New York City. _____

Charting Capital Letters

This chart shows common and proper nouns. Add one more proper noun for each common noun in the chart.

	Common Noun	Proper Noun
people	author	Ginger Gordon _____
	boy	Anthony Reynoso _____
	relative	Dad _____
places	country	Mexico _____
	state	Arizona _____
	city	Guadalupe _____
	street	Elm Street _____
	school	Booker T. Washington Elementary School _____
things	river	Rio Grande _____
	month	September _____
	day	Wednesday _____
	language	Spanish _____

Name _____

Proper Nouns

Remember that titles and their abbreviations, when used with a person's name, begin with a capital letter. Use a capital letter for a person's initials. End abbreviated titles with a period.

Proofread the letter below. Find the proper nouns and titles that need capital letters. Look for abbreviations that need periods. Use the proofreading marks to show the correction.

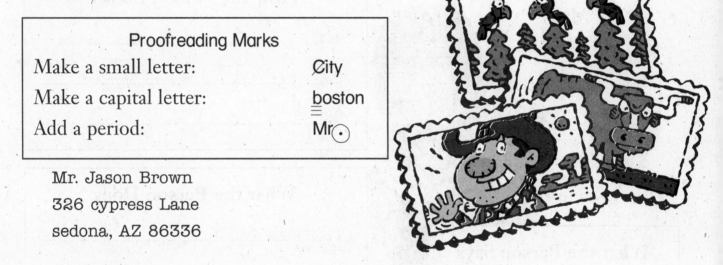

Proofreading Marks	
Make a small letter:	Çity
Make a capital letter:	boston
Add a period:	Mr⊙

Mr. Jason Brown
326 cypress Lane
sedona, AZ 86336

Dear Jason,

Hello from new mexico! I came here with my friend, mrs

williams. We saw some amazing rope tricks at the rodeo. The

winner of the contest was sheriff paul ortega.

After the rodeo, we saw some real animals at the santa fe

National Forest. Our tour guide was dr angela t. carson.

I can't wait to get home and show our pictures to all of you

in mrs walter's class.

Bye for now,
Martin

A Character Sketch

**Use this page to help you plan a character sketch. Write
whom your character sketch will be about. Then write at least
two interesting details about what the person looks like, what
the person says and does, and how you feel about the person.
The details should help you to describe the person.**

**My
Character**

_____

_____

How the Person Looks

1. _____

2. _____

3. _____

What the Person Does

1. _____

2. _____

3. _____

What the Person Says

1. _____

_____

2. _____

_____

3. _____

_____

My Feelings About the Person

1. _____

2. _____

3. _____

**Write your character sketch on a separate sheet of paper.
Use the details above.**

Name _____

Correcting Run-On Sentences

▶ Two or more sentences that run together
  make a **run-on sentence**.

▶ Correct run-on sentences by making separate sentences.
  Add sentence end marks and capital letters where they are needed.

Run-On Sentence:

My friend Patricia loves to dance, she studies ballet every Saturday.

Corrected Sentences:

My friend Patricia loves to dance. She studies ballet every Saturday.

If the sentence is correct, write *Correct.* **If it is a run-on sentence,
write it as two sentences.**

1. My favorite singer is Gloria Estefan, she sings great songs.

   _____

   _____

2. My father runs a restaurant in town, he's the best cook in the world.

   _____

   _____

3. My mother is a math teacher at Yorkstone High School.

   _____

   _____

4. My sister Tasha loves gymnastics, she does the best cartwheels.

   _____

   _____

Name _____

Word Search

Write the letter of the correct definition next to each word. Then find the words in the puzzle and circle them.

1. wealth _____
2. royalty _____
3. collection _____
4. embroidered _____
5. symbols _____
6. flourish _____

a. decorated by sewing
b. kings and queens
c. lots of money or belongings
d. drawings that stand for something
e. a group of items with something in common
f. a showy waving motion

E	M	B	R	O	I	D	E	R	E	D	D	D
K	J	J	M	F	C	O	Q	W	H	R	G	N
O	L	U	J	Y	R	R	O	Y	A	L	T	Y
R	O	Q	I	P	C	C	O	S	H	T	C	A
X	S	L	D	E	E	O	W	V	E	O	J	N
F	P	X	C	C	O	L	L	E	C	T	O	R
H	L	J	J	M	F	L	O	U	R	I	S	H
L	V	I	M	G	C	E	U	U	N	N	J	B
N	E	F	W	I	M	C	P	W	W	D	J	S
S	S	W	E	A	L	T	H	L	P	Z	K	J
S	E	C	J	W	S	I	J	E	L	M	E	L
W	Y	S	Y	M	B	O	L	S	U	R	Q	W
N	T	R	J	B	V	N	D	Y	Y	S	X	O

Name _____

Cluster Maps

Aunt
Phoebe

adinkra
cloth

Name _____

What the Cloth Says

Complete these sentences about *The Talking Cloth*.

Aunt Phoebe tells Amber about many things. Today they

talk about _____ At one

time, only _____ wore it.

Amber learns that the cloth talks because the colors and

symbols _____. If the cloth is

white, that means _____. If it is blue,

that means _____. The symbols on it

stand for ideas like _____ and

_____.

Aunt Phoebe wraps the cloth around Amber. Now she

feels as if she's an _____ with

_____ gathered

around her.

Name _____

Details for Playing

Read the story. Then complete the chart on the next page.

Not for Sale

As Zack walked along, he passed stores with window displays that didn't interest him. Then he came to a store window full of old, worn things. A strange object caught his eye. The wood was dark and shiny smooth. It was long, about as long as Zack's arm, and had six little bowls along each of its sides. At each end was a larger bowl, which made fourteen little bowls in all.

Curious, Zack went inside for a better look. Noting Zack's interest, the shopkeeper explained that the wooden object was a game board carved by an Ashanti artist in Ghana, Africa. The shopkeeper pulled up two chairs and told Zack to sit down. Then he scooped out some brown seeds from one of the bowls and showed Zack how to play *wari*, an Ashanti board game.

At least once a week Zack stopped by the shop to play *wari* with Mr. Oban, the shopkeeper. Both he and Mr. Oban enjoyed playing. And when they finished, Mr. Oban always put the game board away in the back room. It was no longer for sale.

Theme 2: **Celebrating Traditions**   99

Name _____

Details for Playing

continued

**Complete this chart. List details from
the story "Not for Sale."**

List of Details
the game board
1. _____
2. _____
3. _____
4. _____
Zack's feelings
1. _____
2. _____
Zack's actions
1. _____
2. _____
3. _____
4. _____

Name _____

Shorten It!

A **contraction** is the short way of saying or writing two words.
The apostrophe (') takes the place of one or more letters.
Fill in the spaces below to show how contractions are formed.

1. he   + is   =   _____
2. she   + will   =   _____
3. was   + not   =   _____
4. they + are   =   _____
5. I   + will   =   _____
6. _____   + _____   = it's
7. _____   + _____   = you're
8. _____   + _____   = hasn't
9. _____   + _____   = isn't
10. _____   + _____   = we're

The Talking Cloth

Spelling Three-Letter
Clusters and Unexpected
Consonant Patterns

Three-Letter Clusters

When two or more consonants with different sounds are written together, they form a **consonant cluster**. When you are spelling a word that has a consonant cluster, say the word aloud and listen for the different consonant sounds. Remember, some words begin with the consonant clusters *spr*, *str*, and *thr*.

spring   **str**ong   **thr**ow

Some other words have unexpected spelling patterns.

► A beginning /n/ sound may be spelled *kn*, as in **kn**ee. (The *k* is silent.)

► A beginning /r/ sound may be spelled *wr*, as in **wr**ap. (The *w* is silent.)

► A final /ch/ sound may be spelled *tch*, as in pa**tch**. (The *t* is silent.)

Spelling Words

1. spring
2. knee
3. throw
4. patch
5. strong
6. wrap
7. three
8. watch
9. street
10. know
11. spread
12. write

Write each Spelling Word under its proper category.

Three-Letter Clusters	Unexpected Consonant Patterns
_____	_____
_____	_____
_____	_____
_____	_____
_____	_____

Spelling Spree

Hink Pinks Write the Spelling Word that fits the clue
and rhymes with the given word.

Spelling Words

Example: just-born twins **new** _____ *two*

1. a ball tossed to a baby **low** _____
2. jam or jelly **bread** _____
3. cord for a kite on a day in May _____ **string**
4. you and two friends on a school
   holiday _____ **free**
5. a tidy block to live on **neat** _____
6. plastic covering on a bottle top **cap** _____

1. spring
2. knee
3. throw
4. patch
5. strong
6. wrap
7. three
8. watch
9. street
10. know
11. spread
12. write

1. _____   4. _____

2. _____   5. _____

3. _____   6. _____

Finding Words Write the Spelling Words
in each of these words.

7. patchwork _____

8. headstrong _____

9. kneecap _____

10. wristwatch _____

11. knowing _____

12. writer _____

Name _____

Proofreading and Writing

Proofreading Circle the five misspelled Spelling
Words in this character sketch. Then write each
word correctly on the lines below.

1. spring
2. knee
3. throw
4. patch
5. strong
6. wrap
7. three
8. watch
9. street
10. know
11. spread
12. write

Amber's aunt has been everywhere. Aunt
Phoebe takes a long trip to a faraway place every
springe. She has been to Africa thee times. When
she visits a foreign country, she wants to nowe what it
is like to live there. Every time she walks down a new
street, she likes to wache the people carefully. She
notices how they dress and listens to how they speak.
Later, she always takes the time to rite to Amber
about her experiences. I admire Aunt Phoebe because
she is always learning something new.

1. _____   4. _____

2. _____   5. _____

3. _____

Write a Thank-You Note Has a relative or friend ever given
you a special or unusual gift? What was it that made it special?

On a separate sheet of paper, write a thank-you note for the
gift. Make sure to tell the person you are thanking why the gift
is special to you. Use Spelling Words from the list.

Name _____

Rhyming Crossword

Complete the crossword puzzle by writing the correct rhyme for each word. Remember that a rhyming word has the same end sound as another word. Choose your answers from the words in the box.

Vocabulary

trip
map
lace
cause
wealth
silk
smiles
sled
smells
might

Across

2. Object used to go across snow. Rhymes with *said*.
3. A happy person does this. Rhymes with *miles*.
7. A piece of string used to tie a shoe. Rhymes with *face*.
8. Riches. Rhymes with *health*.
9. A voyage. Rhymes with *lip*.
10. Drawings of the earth's surface. Rhymes with *traps*.

Down

1. What your nose does. Rhymes with *tells*.
4. Strength. Rhymes with *right*.
5. A smooth, shiny fabric. Rhymes with *milk*.
6. A reason. Rhymes with *pause*.

Name _____

Circling Nouns

**Circle each singular common noun in the sentences below.
Underline each plural common noun.**

1. Aunt Phoebe collects many things.

2. The cloth is embroidered in sections.

3. The fabric has no patches.

4. The patterns show many colors and shapes.

5. Phoebe gave her niece two boxes.

6. Inside, she found two colorful dresses.

Write each plural noun in the correct column below.

Add -s to form the plural   **Add -es to form the plural**

_____   _____

_____   _____

_____   _____

_____

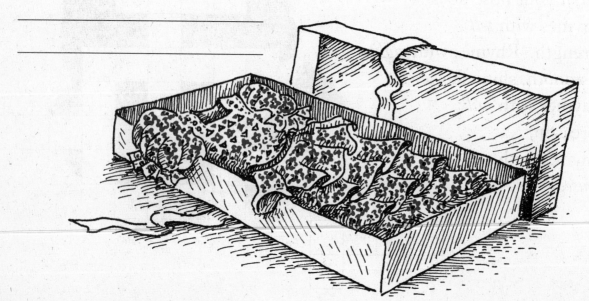

Name _____

Puzzling Plurals

Complete the puzzle by writing the plural of each noun.
Each noun is used only once. Some letters are filled in
to help you get started.

Across		Down	
princess	_____	symbol	_____
basket	_____	box	_____
number	_____	word	_____
thing	_____	pattern	_____
tale	_____	dress	_____

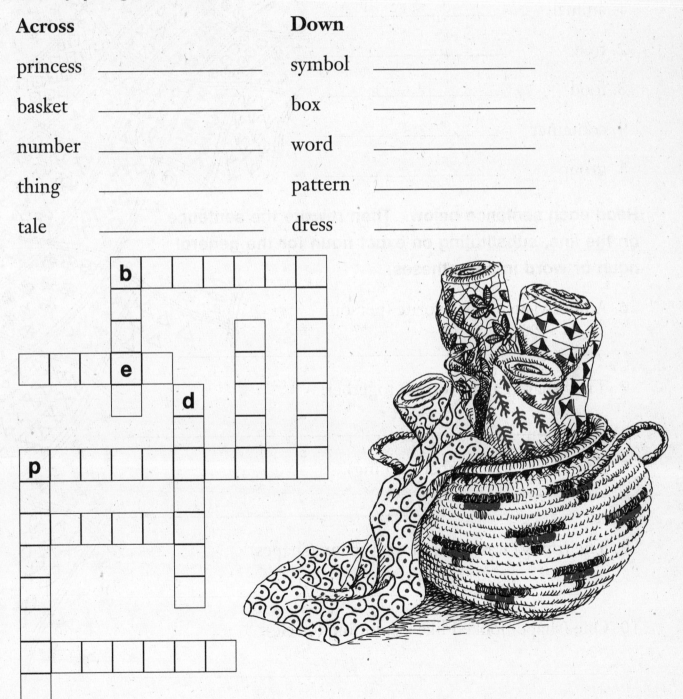

Name _____

Using Exact Nouns

**Write a noun that is more exact than each
general noun below.**

1. animal _____

2. tree _____

3. food _____

4. container _____

5. group _____

**Read each sentence below. Then rewrite the sentence
on the line, substituting an exact noun for the general
noun or word in parentheses.**

6. Amber visited her favorite (person).

_____

7. They shared a hot (drink) together.

_____

8. Phoebe showed Amber a (thing).

_____

9. The (thing) was covered with many (shapes).

_____

10. One (shape) looked like a spinning (circle).

_____

Name _____

Writing an Answer to a Question

When you write an answer to a question, follow these guidelines.

► Read the question carefully.

► Look for key words to help you decide what information the question is asking for.

► Give facts and examples that provide the information asked for.

For each question, write your answer on the lines. Write the start of the answer on the first answer line. Write the rest of the answer on the other answer lines.

1. **Question:** What holiday do you enjoy most? Explain why.
   Turn the question into a statement.

   _____

   Give facts that answer the question.

   _____

   _____

2. **Question:** What place would you like to visit most? Explain why.
   Turn the question into a statement.

   _____

   Give facts that answer the question.

   _____

   _____

Name _____

Writing Complete Sentences

A complete sentence contains both a naming part
and an action part.

Naming Part	Action Part
Aunt Phoebe	bought the adinkra cloth in Africa.

A sentence fragment is an incomplete sentence that has
just one sentence part.

Fragment (naming part only) The Ashanti people.

Fragment (action part only) Made adinkra cloths.

A complete sentence begins with a capital letter and ends
with the correct end punctuation.

**Read each item. Write *Complete Sentence* if the sentence
has both a naming part and an action part. If the item is a
sentence fragment, make it a complete sentence by adding
words. Write your complete sentence correctly.**

1. Means gold or riches. _____

    _____

2. Amber and her father. _____

    _____

3. Aunt Phoebe tells stories to Amber. _____

    _____

4. Drinks hot mocha. _____

    _____

Name _____

What Do You Think?

Answer the questions below. Use your glossary if you need help.

1. Who are some of your ancestors? Where did they live?

   _____

   _____

2. What could someone do to honor his or her

   parents or family members?

   _____

   _____

3. What is something you have learned by imitating another

   person?

   _____

   _____

4. What can you do to show respect for your teacher?

   _____

   _____

5. How should young people act toward their elders?

   _____

   _____

Name _____

Cluster Diagram

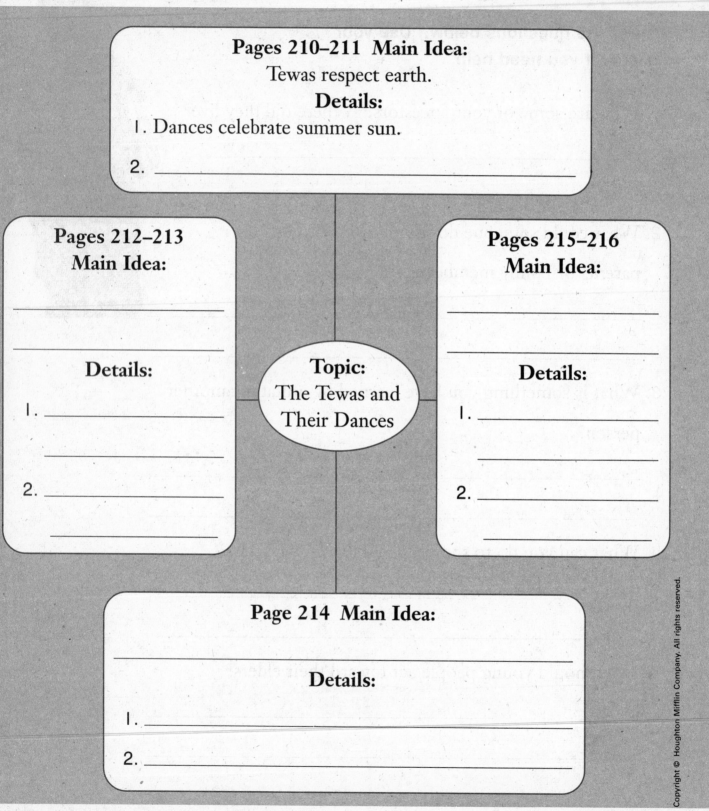

Pages 210–211 Main Idea:
Tewas respect earth.
Details:
1. Dances celebrate summer sun.

2. _____

**Pages 212–213
Main Idea:**

_____
_____
Details:

1. _____
_____

2. _____
_____

Topic:
The Tewas and
Their Dances

**Pages 215–216
Main Idea:**

_____
_____
Details:

1. _____
_____

2. _____
_____

Page 214 Main Idea:

_____
Details:

1. _____

2. _____

Name _____

Feast Day Questions

**Answer each question about *Dancing Rainbows*.
Use complete sentences.**

1. What is Feast Day?

_____

_____

_____

2. Why do Curt, Andy, and the other Tewa people dance on Feast Day?

_____

_____

3. What sounds might you hear on Feast Day in the plaza?

_____

_____

4. When the Tewas dance, what might you see?

_____

_____

_____

5. What did Andy do for his grandson and other young Tewas?

_____

_____

Name _____

Mainly Ideas

**Read the article. Then complete the diagram on
the next page.**

All About Eagles

How many different kinds of eagles do you think live in
the world? If you guessed about sixty, you'd be right. Some
kinds of eagles are large and some are small. Most are strong
for their size. Some are even strong enough to lift
food weighing almost as much as they do!

Eagles have been used as symbols of power and
freedom. Some people call them the "king of birds"
because of their strength and brave,
proud looks. In 1782, the United
States of America chose the bald
eagle as its national bird.

Bald eagles are among the
larger eagles. They can weigh
anywhere from eight to thirteen
pounds. These great birds can
have wings that spread as much as
seven feet across! Their heads are
covered with white feathers,
making them look "bald" from
a distance.

Name _____

Mainly Ideas continued

Complete the diagram with facts from "All About Eagles."

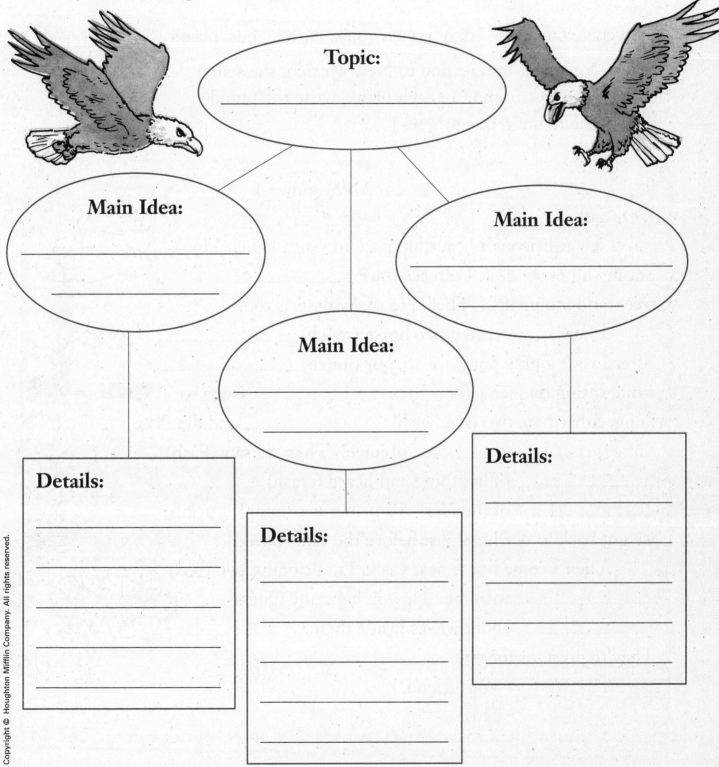

Topic:
_____

Main Idea:
_____
_____

Main Idea:
_____
_____

Main Idea:
_____

Details:
_____
_____
_____
_____

Details:
_____
_____
_____
_____

Details:
_____
_____
_____

Dancing Rainbows

Structural Analysis
Plurals of Words Ending in
ch, sh, x, s

Name _____

More and More Plurals

Add *-es* to form the plural of a singular noun that ends in *ch*, *sh*, *x*, or *s*.

  branch/branch**es**   dish/dish**es**   mix/mix**es**   bus/bus**es**

When Dora went on vacation to New Mexico, she sent a letter to her best friend. In each blank, write the plural form of the noun in parentheses ( ).

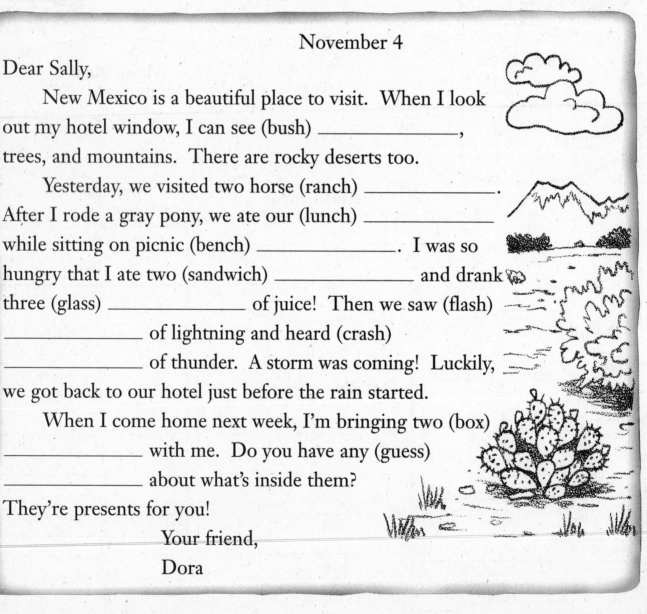

November 4

Dear Sally,

New Mexico is a beautiful place to visit. When I look out my hotel window, I can see (bush) _____, trees, and mountains. There are rocky deserts too.

Yesterday, we visited two horse (ranch) _____. After I rode a gray pony, we ate our (lunch) _____ while sitting on picnic (bench) _____. I was so hungry that I ate two (sandwich) _____ and drank three (glass) _____ of juice! Then we saw (flash) _____ of lightning and heard (crash) _____ of thunder. A storm was coming! Luckily, we got back to our hotel just before the rain started.

When I come home next week, I'm bringing two (box) _____ with me. Do you have any (guess) _____ about what's inside them? They're presents for you!

Your friend,

Dora

Name _____

The Long *i* Sound

When you hear the /ī/ sound, think of the patterns *igh*, *i*, and *ie*.

/ī/ br**igh**t, w**i**ld, d**ie**

Write each Spelling Word under its spelling of the /ī/ sound.

Spelling Words

1. wild
2. bright
3. die
4. sight
5. child
6. pie
7. fight
8. lie
9. tight
10. tie
11. might
12. mind

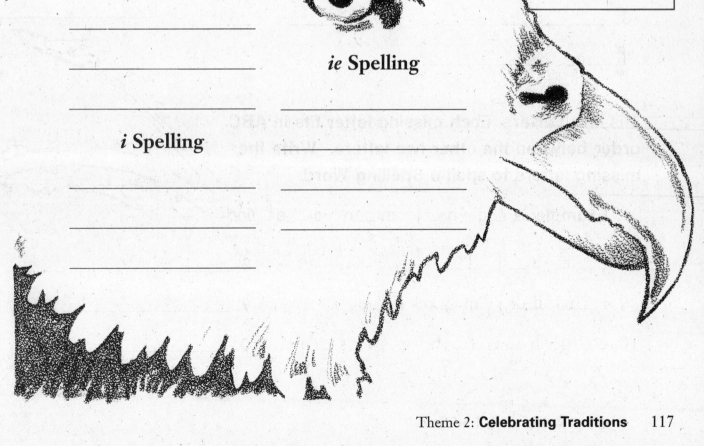

igh **Spelling**

_____

_____

_____

_____

ie **Spelling**

_____

i **Spelling**

_____

_____

_____

Name _____

Spelling Spree

Sentence Pairs Write the Spelling Word that best completes each pair of sentences.

Example: A jet does not fly low. It flies _high_ .

1. These shoes are not loose. They are _____.
2. My sister is not a grownup. She is a _____.
3. A tiger is not tame. It is _____.
4. I will not have cake for dessert. I will have _____.
5. Neither team won. The score was a _____.
6. The sunshine is not dim today. It is _____.
7. He did not tell the truth. He told a_____.

1. _____   5. _____

2. _____   6. _____

3. _____   7. _____

4. _____

Missing Letters Each missing letter fits in ABC order between the other two letters. Write the missing letters to spell a Spelling Word.

Example: e _ g   h _ j   m _ o   c _ e   *find*

8. c _ e   h _ j   d _ f   8. _____

9. l _ n   h _ j   m _ o   c _ e   9. _____

10. e _ g   h _ j   f _ h   g _ i   s _ u   10. _____

Name _____

Proofreading and Writing

Proofreading Circle the five misspelled Spelling Words in this page from a travel brochure. Then write each word correctly.

Visit Beautiful New Mexico!

Come to New Mexico and discover a land of amazing beauty! Explore wonderful deserts bathed in brit sunshine. Hike in our mountains and experience adventure in the wilde! Relax your minde and body at one of our many resorts. Enjoy the siet of colorful hot-air balloons in Albuquerque. Spend a week with us, and you just mieght never go home again! That's no lie.

Spelling Words

1. wild
2. bright
3. die
4. sight
5. child
6. pie
7. fight
8. lie
9. tight
10. tie
11. might
12. mind

1. _____   3. _____   5. _____

2. _____   4. _____

Write an Explanation The Tewas believe that the eagle is a special animal that carries messages to earth. If you could wear an animal costume, what animal would you choose to be?

On a separate sheet of paper, tell what animal you would choose and explain why you think this animal is special. Use Spelling Words from the list.

Name _____

Definition Derby

Read the dictionary entry for the word *dance*. Then write sample sentences as directed.

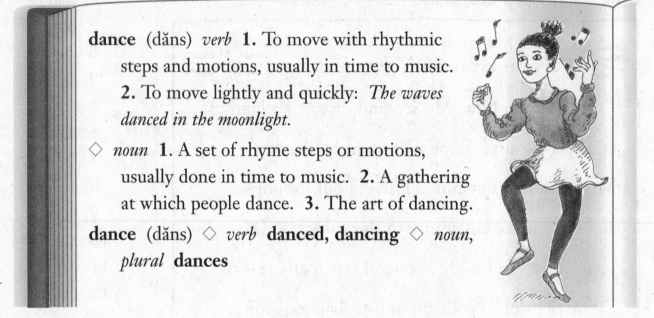

dance (dăns) *verb* **1.** To move with rhythmic steps and motions, usually in time to music. **2.** To move lightly and quickly: *The waves danced in the moonlight.*
◇ *noun* **1.** A set of rhyme steps or motions, usually done in time to music. **2.** A gathering at which people dance. **3.** The art of dancing.
dance (dăns) ◇ *verb* **danced, dancing** ◇ *noun, plural* **dances**

1. Write a sentence using the most common meaning of *dance*.

_____

2. Write a sentence using noun definition number 3.

_____

3. Write a sentence using noun definition number 1.

_____

4. Write a sentence using verb definition number 2.

_____

5. Write a sentence using the least common meaning of *dance*.

_____

120   Theme 2: **Celebrating Traditions**

Name _____

Beat the Drum for Plurals

Circle all the plural nouns and write each one in the correctly labeled drum.

1. The Tewa children practice dancing.
2. Men and women prepare for a festival.
3. The skies are clear and blue.
4. Families arrive from many different cities.
5. The parties are about to begin.
6. Loaves of bread are stacked on the table.
7. People stomp their feet.
8. Sweet candies are a special treat.

Change _y_ to _i_ and add -_es_

_____

_____

_____

_____

Special Plural Forms

_____

_____

_____

_____

Name _____

Completing with Plurals

Complete the story by writing the plural form for each noun in parentheses.

1. The _____ are sunny and clear. (sky)

2. All the relatives help bake many _____ of bread for the feast. (loaf)

3. Many _____ have come to the celebration. (family)

4. At last, six _____ begin to dance. (man)

5. Their _____ fly above the ground. (foot)

122   Theme 2: **Celebrating Traditions**

Proofreading for Noun Endings

Proofread the paragraphs below. Find plurals of nouns that are spelled incorrectly. Circle each misspelled plural. Then write each correctly spelled noun on the lines below. Use a dictionary for help.

> After sunrise, the Tewa mens and womens gather.
> Mothers carry their smiling babys. Fatheres walk with
> their sons and daughters. People arrive from many citys.
> They look forward to the dances and the storys.
>
> Three childs wear buffalo costumies. They are
> dancers. Their feet move in beautiful patternes. After the
> dance, everyone feasts on loafs of bread and tasty treats.

Regular	Ends in consonant + *y*	Special plurals
_____	_____	_____
_____	_____	_____
_____	_____	_____
		_____

Name _____

Writing a News Article

Use this page to plan and organize your news article about a holiday or celebration. When you finish, use the outline to write your article on a separate sheet of paper.

1. Holiday or Celebration _____

_____

2. Who? _____

_____

3. What? _____

_____

4. When? _____

_____

5. Where? _____

_____

6. Why? _____

_____

7. How? _____

_____

8. Interesting Opening Sentence _____

_____

9. Interesting Headline _____

Name _____

Newspaper Article

Audience A good newspaper article includes details that help
the audience picture what they did not witness themselves.

**Read the newspaper article. Then answer each question
based on some facts or details from the article.**

> In the past month, San Juan Pueblo has had no rain. The
> elders of the Tewa tribe who live there have decided to hold a
> rain dance. The dancing will begin at nine in the morning and
> last until noon. The purpose of the dance is to ask the Tewa
> ancestors to bring rain. Andy Garcia is an elder of the tribe.
> He says that the Tewa believe that their ancestors come back as
> raindrops to water their crops and give them water to drink.

1. Who are the Tewa?

   _____

2. Where will the rain dance be held?

   _____

3. What would make an interesting beginning to the article?

   _____

   _____

   _____

4. What would make an interesting headline for this article?

   _____

**Congratulations! You are a good reporter! Now write your new,
improved article on a separate piece of paper.**

Name _____

Filling in the Blank

Use the test-taking strategies and tips you have learned to help you complete fill-in-the-blank items about *The Keeping Quilt*. This practice will help you when you take this kind of test.

Read each item. At the bottom of the page, fill in the circle for the answer that best completes the sentence.

1 **By pointing out that Anna was speaking English in only six months while her parents never learned much of it, the author shows that —**

   Ⓐ Anna was smarter than her parents

   Ⓑ it is easier for young people to learn a new language

   Ⓒ it is important for children to go to school

   Ⓓ Anna's parents wanted to move back to Russia

2 **The author probably believes that it is important to remember your homeland, because in the story she has —**

   Ⓕ Anna's parents speak Russian rather than English

   Ⓖ the neighborhood ladies cut out animals and flowers for the quilt

   Ⓗ a detailed description of Anna's home in Russia

   Ⓙ Anna want a quilt to remind the family of Russia

ANSWER ROWS   I Ⓐ Ⓑ Ⓒ Ⓓ   2 Ⓕ Ⓖ Ⓗ Ⓙ

Name _____

Filling in the Blank continued

3 The quilt is not always mentioned in the story, but the author lets the reader know how special it is to Anna by having pictures that show —

   Ⓐ the quilt at important events in Anna's life

   Ⓑ Anna giving it to her husband as a gift

   Ⓒ the quilt as the background in every scene

   Ⓓ how Anna makes it into something new and different as she gets older

4 The author has Mary Ellen tell her daughter about the pieces of cloth that went into making the quilt to —

   Ⓕ encourage Patricia to make her own quilt

   Ⓖ describe how the quilt was made

   Ⓗ teach Patricia about her family

   Ⓙ explain to Patricia how to recycle old clothes

5 The author ends the story by saying "Traci and Steven were now all grownup and getting ready to start their own lives," so the reader knows that —

   Ⓐ the family doesn't need the quilt anymore

   Ⓑ the quilt will continue to be used

   Ⓒ the author plans to write another book about the quilt

   Ⓓ the quilt is too old and worn out for Traci and Steven

ANSWER ROWS   3 Ⓐ Ⓑ Ⓒ Ⓓ   5 Ⓐ Ⓑ Ⓒ Ⓓ
                4 Ⓕ Ⓖ Ⓗ Ⓙ

Name _____

Spelling Review

Write Spelling Words from the list to answer the questions.

1–9. Which nine words have the long *a* or long *e* sound?

1. _____   6. _____

2. _____   7. _____

3. _____   8. _____

4. _____   9. _____

5. _____

10–16. Which seven words have the long *o* sound?

10. _____   14. _____

11. _____   15. _____

12. _____   16. _____

13. _____

17–22. Which six words have the long *i* sound?

17. _____   20. _____

18. _____   21. _____

19. _____   22. _____

23–25. Which three words end with these letters?

23. _____tch   24. _____ead   25. _____ap

23. _____   25. _____

24. _____

Spelling Words

1. lay
2. feel
3. hold
4. wild
5. might
6. paint
7. seem
8. patch
9. three
10. own
11. speak
12. need
13. lie
14. most
15. spread
16. float
17. row
18. leave
19. both
20. wrap
21. know
22. mind
23. street
24. bright
25. tie

Name _____

Spelling Spree

Rhyme Time Write the Spelling Word that rhymes with the word in dark print.

Example: A plump kitty is a ___fat___ **cat.**

1. A nice brain is a **kind** _____.

2. An animal life jacket is a **goat** _____.

3. An unreal piece of clothing is a _____ **lie.**

4. Baby triplets are a **wee** _____.

Word Search Underline the eight hidden Spelling Words. Then write the words.

Example: abeneedlean ___needle___

5. redawildell

6. ymightaledfl

7. enrstreetalp

8. knpaintilke

9. teriloneedum

10. grpatchibror

11. olgeraspread

12. wrilleavekn

5. _____

6. _____

7. _____

8. _____

9. _____

10. _____

11. _____

12. _____

Spelling Words
1. paint
2. leave
3. might
4. need
5. mind
6. tie
7. spread
8. float
9. three
10. wild
11. patch
12. street

Name _____

Proofreading and Writing

Proofreading Circle the six misspelled Spelling Words in this play. Then write each word correctly.

Grandpa: Let's rapp the gifts in brite yellow paper.

Joe: We can laye it on the table for Mom.

Grandpa: Be careful how you hoald it.

Joe: You kno we bouth did a good job!

1. _____   3. _____   5. _____

2. _____   4. _____   6. _____

Complete a Letter Use Spelling Words to complete the following letter.

Thanksgiving makes me 7. _____ very

happy. Our family has its 8. _____ traditions.

My grandfather will 9. _____ his 10. _____

about sharing with others. A feast will 11. _____

on the table, with many plates in a 12. _____.

The 13. _____ simple dishes 14. _____

even tastier then.

Write a Description On a separate sheet of paper, describe a celebration you enjoy. Use the Spelling Words.

Spelling Words

1. lay
2. most
3. wrap
4. lie
5. feel
6. seem
7. hold
8. speak
9. own
10. bright
11. row
12. both
13. know
14. mind

Name _____

It's Tricky!

Compare the three trickster tales.

▶ Draw a cover cartoon for each tale.

▶ Write enough about the story to make someone want to read it.

For example:

Rabbit races Turtle.

But in the end, Turtle wins!

How does slow Turtle beat

fast Rabbit?

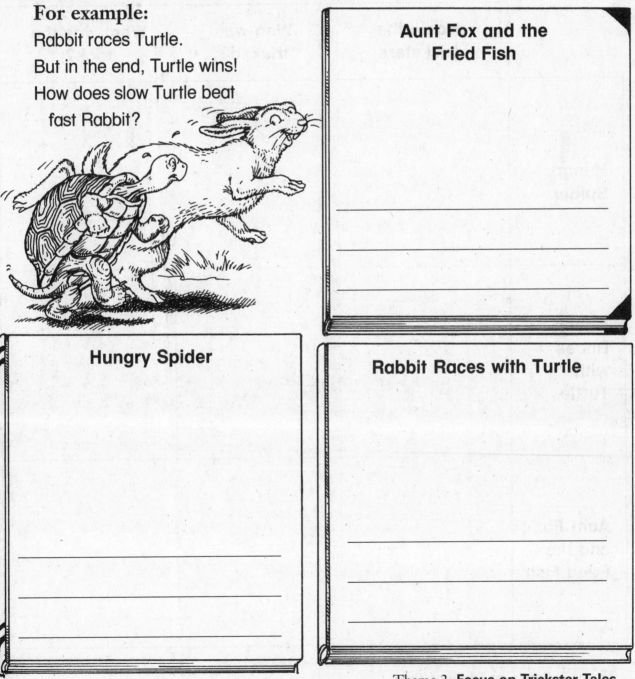

Aunt Fox and the Fried Fish

_____

_____

_____

Hungry Spider

_____

_____

_____

Rabbit Races with Turtle

_____

_____

_____

Name _____

What Makes a Trickster Tale?

After reading each selection, complete the chart below to tell why each story is a trickster tale.

	Name the tricksters	Who was tricked?	What was the trick?
Hungry Spider			
Rabbit Races with Turtle			
Aunt Fox and the Fried Fish			

Name _____

Incredible Stories

What do you think makes a story incredible? Is it the characters, the setting, or the events? Complete the web with words or phrases that describe an incredible story.

Incredible Stories

Now list some books, movies, or real events that you think are incredible.

_____

_____

_____

_____

Name _____

Incredible Stories

Fill in the chart as you read the stories.

	What incredible thing happens?	How do the characters respond?
Dogzilla		
The Mysterious Giant of Barletta		
Raising Dragons		
The Garden of Abdul Gasazi		

Name _____

Monster Words

Circle the two words that are most alike in meaning.

1. colossal
   small
   big

2. animal
   creature
   tree

3. strong
   brave
   heroic

4. huge
   monstrous
   bad

5. enormous
   terrifying
   scary

6. tremendous
   tiny
   large

7. frightening
   fun
   horrifying

8. little
   tremendous
   colossal

9. terrifying
   horrifying
   monstrous

10. colossal
    heroic
    monstrous

Fantasy and Realism Chart

Story Events and Characters	Fantasy (Make Believe)	Realism (True-to-Life)
	1. A city is built and run _____ _____ _____	1. The wind carries the scent _____ _____
	2. _____ _____ _____	2. _____ _____
	3. _____ _____ _____	3. _____ _____ _____
	4. _____ _____ _____	4. _____ _____
	5. _____ _____ _____	5. _____ _____

Name _____

Fix the Facts

Read this newspaper story about *Dogzilla*, and draw a line through the mistakes. Then write what really happened.

Monster Makes News!

The people in Mousopolis took part in a Cook-Off. It was winter, and smoke lifted over the city. Soon a strange sound was heard: "Quack . . . quack." Then Dogzilla climbed out of a cave!

The troops were sent out. But Dogzilla hid, and the troops danced home. Dogzilla wandered the city looking for a place to sleep. The mice called a meeting. The mice decided the only way to defeat Dogzilla was to think like a donkey. So they munched grass and waited. It worked! Dogzilla ran out of town. And the problem was solved forever.

_____

_____

_____

_____

_____

_____

_____

A Real Fantasy

**Read the story. Find parts that are fantasy
and parts that could happen in real life.**

A Fish Tale

Way up north, it's cold and dark for much of the year.
But that's how polar bears like it, or at least, that's what
people think.

"I hate the cold and dark," said Ursa Bear from her seat by
the fire. "I want to go where it's warm!"

"That's silly!" snapped her sister. "Now go catch some
fish for dinner."

Soon Ursa sat by the ocean's edge, waiting. Her first catch
was a mackerel with shiny scales.

"Please don't eat me," begged the fish. "If you let me go,
I'll grant you one wish!"

"Can you do that?" asked Ursa. "Then I wish I were
somewhere sunny and warm! Here, my friend, I'll let you go."

At once Ursa found herself on a sunny beach next to some
surprised people. "This is great!" she cried. "Now where can I
find a beach chair?"

The mackerel was even happier. "That's the tenth bear
I've wished away today!" he laughed. "Soon my fish friends
and I will be all by ourselves."

Name _____

A Real Fantasy continued

Finish the chart. List five fantasy details and five realistic details from the story.

Fantasy Details (make-believe)	Realistic Details (true-to-life)
1. _____ _____	1. _____ _____
2. _____ _____	2. _____ _____
3. _____ _____	3. _____ _____
4. _____ _____	4. _____ _____
5. _____ _____	5. _____ _____

Dogzilla

Structural Analysis Forming
Plurals of Nouns Ending in
f or *fe*

Name _____

Plurals Puzzle

Write the plural noun that matches each clue in the puzzle.
Use the Word Bank and a dictionary for help.

Word Bank

thief	cliff	life	safe	wolf
wife	calf	shelf	belief	half

Across
1. Wild animals
2. Young cows
3. Ledges to hold things
5. People who steal
8. Opinions

Down
1. Married women
2. Steep rock walls
4. A cat has nine of these
6. Two equal parts of a whole
7. Containers used for protecting valuable items

Name _____

The Vowel Sounds in *clown* and *lawn*

The /ou/ sound you hear in *clown* can be spelled with the pattern *ow* or *ou*. The /ô/ sound you hear in *lawn* can be spelled with these patterns: *aw*, *o*, or *a* before *l*.

/ou/ cl**ow**n, s**ou**nd

/ô/ l**aw**n, cl**o**th, t**a**lk

▶ In the starred word *would*, *ou* does not spell the /ou/ sound. Instead, *ou* spells the vowel sound you hear in the word *book*.

Write each Spelling Word under its vowel sound.

1. clown
2. lawn
3. talk
4. sound
5. cloth
6. would*
7. also
8. mouth
9. crown
10. soft
11. count
12. law

/ou/ Sound

_____

_____

_____

_____

_____

/ô/ Sound

_____

_____

_____

_____

_____

_____

_____

Another Vowel Sound

_____

Name _____

Spelling Spree

Hidden Words Write the Spelling Word that is
hidden in each group of letters. Do not let the
other letters fool you.

Example: e t i t o w n p e *town*

1. p r e s o f t a c _____

2. c h a l s o g h e r _____

3. l a n r c l o t h _____

4. r e c l o w n e f _____

Spelling Words

1. clown
2. lawn
3. talk
4. sound
5. cloth
6. would*
7. also
8. mouth
9. crown
10. soft
11. count
12. law

Letter Swap Change the underlined letter in each
word to make a Spelling Word. Write the Spelling
Word.

Example: s<u>h</u>all *small*

5. co<u>u</u>rt _____

6. <u>d</u>awn _____

7. crow<u>s</u> _____

8. <u>s</u>outh _____

9. tal<u>l</u> _____

10. wo<u>r</u>ld _____

11. l<u>o</u>w _____

12. <u>m</u>ound _____

Name _____

Proofreading and Writing

Proofreading Circle the five misspelled Spelling
Words. Then write each word correctly.

WARNING TO MICE!

The monster has had puppies! At last cownt,

six had been seen. They are now in the city.

Do not think of these dogs as sawft and cute.

They tore up a laun! They chewed up some

kloth! Many mice woud fit in one puppy's

mouth. So if you see one, run!

Spelling Words

1. clown
2. lawn
3. talk
4. sound
5. cloth
6. would*
7. also
8. mouth
9. crown
10. soft
11. count
12. law

1. _____   4. _____

2. _____   5. _____

3. _____

Write a Comparison How big is a mouse? How big
is a dog? What does a mouse eat? What does a dog
eat? How many feet does each animal have? What are
their tails like?

**On a separate piece of paper, write a comparison of
a dog and a mouse. Tell how they are alike and how
they are different. Use Spelling Words from the list.**

Find Meaning Using Context

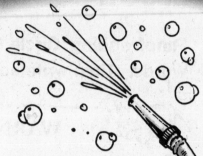

Choose the correct definition for each of the underlined words in the passage. Write the letter of the definition after the number of the word it matches. Use context clues to help you.

a. ran away, fled
b. frightened, alarmed
c. helpful, constructive
d. enjoyment, pleasure
e. shiver or shake

f. relating to a very early time before events were written down
g. carved, as a design on metal or glass

h. very bad, terrible
i. extremely deep place
j. call forth, gather together

    All at once, the volcano began to <u>tremble</u> and rumble. Up from the <u>depths</u> of the earth came the <u>dreadful</u> Dogzilla! This monster was millions of years old, from <u>prehistoric</u> times. The mice didn't think they could teach it to do anything <u>positive</u> for their town. Using all the courage they could <u>muster</u>, the mice approached Dogzilla. They hit her with a blast of warm, sudsy water. The <u>panicking</u> pooch took off at <u>top speed</u>. Delighted, the Big Cheese watched with <u>relish</u> as Dogzilla <u>hightailed</u> it out of town. The scary memory of the bubble bath was <u>etched</u> in Dogzilla's mind forever.

1. _____   4. _____   7. _____

2. _____   5. _____   8. _____   10. _____

3. _____   6. _____   9. _____

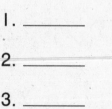

Name _____

Writing Possessive Nouns

Rewrite each phrase, using a possessive.

1. the barbecue of the mouse

_____

2. the behavior of the animal

_____

3. the barbecue of the mice

_____

4. the shouts of the mayor

_____

5. the smoke of two volcanoes

_____

6. the shouts of the citizens

_____

7. the tail of the cat

_____

8. the cries of the soldiers

_____

9. the dog belonging to the Smiths

_____

10. the dog belonging to Abigail

_____

Name _____

Finding the Possessive

On the line provided, write the noun in parentheses as a possessive noun to complete each sentence. Then write *S* if the possessive noun is singular, and *P* if it is plural.

1. The _____ pictures dazzle the reader. (artist) ___

2. I think that the _____ interest will be high. (readers) ___

3. An _____ imagination is clear on every page. (illustrator) ___

4. The _____ expression looks like a smile. (dog) ___

5. At the end of the story, the _____ faces are adorable. (puppies) ___

6. Most _____ faces aren't that cute! (monsters) ___

7. Every _____ reaction will be a little different. (reader) ___

8. All of the _____ actions were ridiculous. (characters) ___

9. I think that our _____ favorite character is Dogzilla. (class) ___

10. The book was awarded a prize by the _____ committee. (teachers) ___

Name _____

Apostrophes

**Rewrite each of the following sentences, adding
apostrophes to each incorrectly spelled possessive noun.**

1. How would Dav Pilkeys book be different if it were called *Frogzilla*?

_____

_____

2. The city would be crushed by Frogzillas huge feet.

_____

_____

3. The new heros name might be Dennis the Fly.

_____

_____

4. What do you think the flys strategy would be?

_____

_____

5. What are the frogs weaknesses?

_____

_____

Name _____

Writing a Journal Entry

In the space below, write a journal entry for today. Describe things you see, feel, think about, or remember. Then use your entry to complete the table below.

My Daily Journal

Today's Date: _____

_____

_____

_____

_____

_____

_____

_____

What I Wrote About Today

Facts	Observations	Feelings	Memories	Ideas

Name _____

Voice

Suppose one of the puppies wrote this journal entry:

Those silly mice! They think their big barbecue tommorow will go off without a hitch. Well, they've had their peace and quiet. Now let's see if they like to play with puppys! I'm raring to go, and I'm planning on having lots of fun in Mousopolis tomorrow. And if they tries any of that bath stuff on me, we'll just see who can take a licking!

Suppose the Big Cheese wrote this in his journal:

Tomorrow is the first anniversary of the Dogzilla disaster, and that makes me nervous. What hapened to Dogzilla? Can we be sure she don't come back? Will tomorrow be the day a new monster destroies poor Mousopolis yet again? I'm scared!

1. How would you describe the puppy's voice in his entry?

_____

_____

2. How would you describe the Big Cheese's voice in his entry?

_____

_____

In both journal entries, circle examples of grammar and spelling that are not perfect.

Name _____

Revising Your Story

Reread your story. What do you need to make it better? Use this page to help you decide. Put a checkmark in the box for each sentence that describes your personal narrative.

Rings the Bell!

☐ The beginning catches the reader's interest.

☐ My plot is well developed and will hold the reader's attention.

☐ My characters are interesting. I used many details.

☐ I told enough so the reader can picture the setting.

☐ There are almost no mistakes.

Getting Stronger

☐ The beginning could be more interesting.

☐ My plot isn't always clear. Some parts need more explanation.

☐ The ending doesn't really tell how the problem was solved.

☐ I need to add more details.

☐ There are a few mistakes.

Try Harder

☐ The beginning is boring.

☐ The problem is not clear. I did not tell how it was solved.

☐ I need details that tell about my character and the setting.

Name _____

Using Possessive Nouns

A **possessive noun** shows ownership.

▶ Add *'s* to make a noun possessive.

▶ Add just an **'** (apostrophe) to make a plural
noun that ends with *s* a possessive noun.

**Rewrite each phrase, using a possessive noun. Then use
the new phrase in a sentence of your own.**

1. the equipment of the team _____

_____

_____

2. the teamwork of the players _____

_____

_____

3. the orders of the coach _____

_____

_____

4. the roar of the audience _____

_____

_____

5. the songs of the cheerleaders _____

_____

_____

Name _____

Spelling Words

Look for spelling patterns you have learned to help you remember the Spelling Words on this page. Think about the parts that you find hard to spell.

Write the missing letters in the Spelling Words below.

1. and
2. said
3. goes
4. going
5. some
6. something
7. you
8. your
9. friend
10. school
11. where
12. myself

1. an _____

2. s _____ _____ d

3. go _____

4. go _____ _____ _____

5. s _____ me

6. som _____ thing

7. y _____ _____

8. y _____ _____ _____

9. fr _____ _____ nd

10. s _____ _____ ool

11. w _____ ere

12. m _____ _____ elf

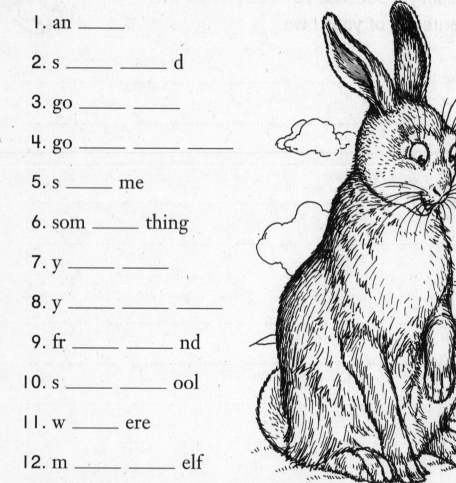

Study List On another sheet of paper, write each Spelling Word. Check the list to be sure you spell each word correctly.

Name _____

Spelling Spree

The Third Word Write the Spelling Word that belongs in each group.

1. I, me, _____

2. plus, also, _____

3. talked, spoke, _____

4. pal, buddy, _____

5. their, our, _____

6. moves, runs, _____

1. and
2. said
3. goes
4. going
5. some
6. something
7. you
8. your
9. friend
10. school
11. where
12. myself

Sentence Fillers Write the Spelling Word that makes the most sense in each sentence below.

7. Do you know _____ soccer practice is tomorrow?

8. I have _____ books about bears that I bought last summer.

9. Our _____ usually lets out at 3 o'clock.

10. When is your class _____ to the library?

11. My brother wrote _____ in my notebook, but I can't read it.

12. Have _____ seen my pet snake anywhere?

Proofreading and Writing

Proofreading Circle the four misspelled Spelling Words in the story. Then write each word correctly.

1. and
2. said
3. goes
4. going
5. some
6. something
7. you
8. your
9. friend
10. school
11. where
12. myself

Yesterday, I was on my way into skool when I heard something rustling in the bushes. I turned around an went over to see what it was. I looked in the spot were I had heard the noise, but there was nothing there. Then, from behind me, a voice sed, "Are you looking for me?" I turned around and found myself face to face with a fox with a sly grin on its face.

1. _____ 3. _____

2. _____ 4. _____

Incredible Sentences Write four sentences that tell about something incredible. Use a Spelling Word from the list in each one.

Name _____

What Do These Words Mean?

Look up each word in your glossary. Then, in the box above each word, draw a picture that shows the meaning of the word.

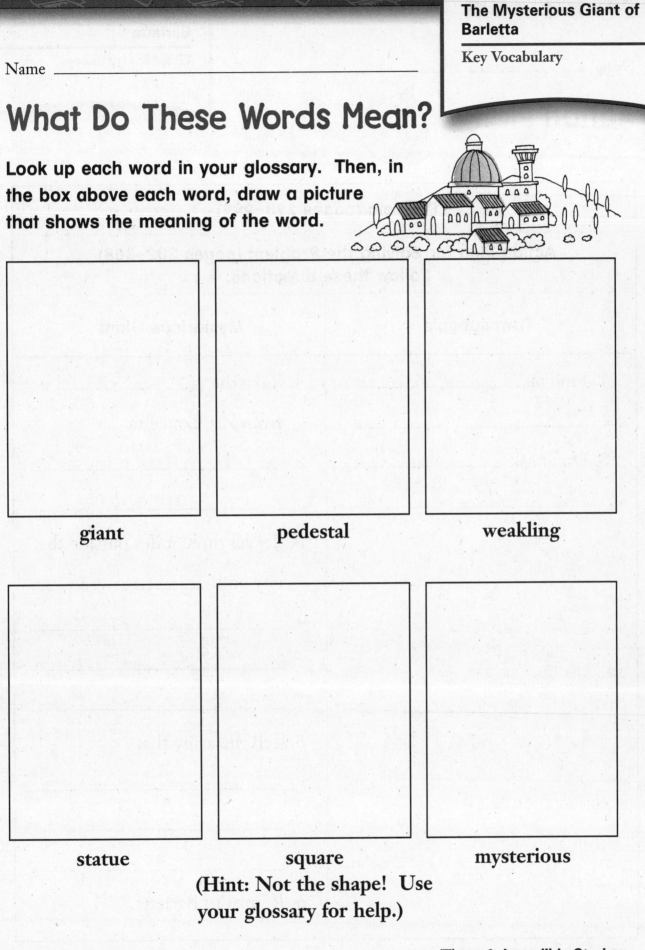

giant

pedestal

weakling

statue

square
(Hint: Not the shape! Use your glossary for help.)

mysterious

Name _____

Action Plan

Problem (pages 298–299)	
Action Plan for Solving the Problem (pages 302–308) Follow these directions:	
Townspeople	**Mysterious Giant**
1. Find an _____.	1. Take the _____ from Zia Concetta.
2. _____	2. _____
3. Don't ask _____ _____.	3. Travel three miles outside the city and _____.
	4. _____ _____ _____
	5. Tell the army that _____ _____ _____.
	6. Return to Barletta.

158   Theme 3: **Incredible Stories**

Name _____

Remember the Details

Think about *The Mysterious Giant of Barletta*. **Then complete the sentences.**

1. The people of Barletta show their love for the Mysterious Giant by

   _____

   _____

2. The peaceful time for Barletta is over when

   _____

   _____

3. Zia Concetta and the Giant figure out a plan to save Barletta. The plan is

   _____

   _____

4. After the soldiers hear what the Giant says, they wonder

   _____

   _____

5. The army captain decides there is only one thing to do, so they

   _____

   _____

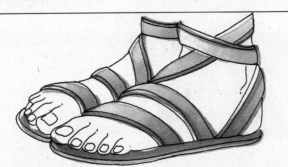

Name _____

Directions for Fun

Read the directions. Then answer the questions on the next page.

Fingertip Puppets

Act out your favorite folktale or story using puppets you've made yourself. It's easy and fun to do. All you need are an old rubber glove, scissors, glue, marking pens, and some craft supplies.

First, find an old rubber glove that can be cut apart. Each finger will become a puppet. Draw a line about 2 ½ inches below each fingertip of the glove. Cut along the line and then turn the fingertip inside out.

Next, make the puppet look special. Draw a funny face on your puppet. Then glue on hair made from cotton or yarn. Finally, glue on a hat, shirt, or collar made with pieces of felt. You may also want to add beads, buttons, or trims.

Name _____

Directions for Fun continued

Answer each question about making a fingertip puppet.

1. What supplies will you need?

_____

_____

2. After you find an old rubber glove, what do you do?

_____

_____

3. Why should you draw the line before you cut?

_____

_____

4. After you cut off the fingertip, what should you do next?

_____

_____

5. What should you do before you glue on the hair?

_____

_____

Name _____

Giant Endings

**Fill in each blank using the base word and the ending -er or
-est. The base words are in dark type. To solve the puzzle,
write the numbered letter from each answer on the line with
the matching number.**

1. The statue was the ___ ___ ___ ___ ___ ___ ___ thing
   5

   in Barletta. (**tall**)

2. The statue had been in the square ___ ___ ___ ___ ___ ___
                                                            7

   than anyone could remember. (**long**)

3. To the Giant, late nights were the ___ ___ ___ ___ ___
                                          1

   time of all. (**nice**)

4. The town was ___ ___ ___ ___ ___ ___ ___ at night
                     3

   than at any other time. (**quiet**)

5. The army was ___ ___ ___ ___ ___ ___ ___ ___ than
                        2   6

   the people of Barletta. (**strong**)

6. The torches were ___ ___ ___ ___ ___ ___ ___ ___
                                                  4

   than ever. (**bright**)

The Mysterious Giant has a lot of:

___ ___ ___ ___ ___ ___ ___
 1   2   3   4   5   6   7

Name _____

Vowel + /r/ Sounds

Remember these spelling patterns for the vowel + /r/ sounds:

Patterns		Examples
/är/	**ar**	dark
/îr/	**ear**	clear
/ôr/	**or**	north
/ûr/	**er**	her
	ir	girl
	ur	turn
	or	work

Write each Spelling Word under its vowel + /r/ sounds.

Spelling Words

1. girl
2. clear
3. her
4. turn
5. dark
6. work
7. smart
8. word
9. hurt
10. serve
11. north
12. third

/är/ Sounds

_____

_____

/îr/ Sounds

_____

_____

/ôr/ Sounds

_____

_____

/ûr/ Sounds

_____

_____

_____

_____

_____

_____

Spelling Spree

Questions Write a Spelling Word to answer each question.

1. What direction is opposite to south?
2. How do you feel when you solve a hard problem?
3. What might a car do at a street corner?
4. What do you call a sky without clouds?
5. What is it like outside after sunset?
6. What comes between second and fourth?

1. _____   4. _____

2. _____   5. _____

3. _____   6. _____

1. girl
2. clear
3. her
4. turn
5. dark
6. work
7. smart
8. word
9. hurt
10. serve
11. north
12. third

Missing Letters Each missing letter fits in ABC order between the other letters. Write the missing letters to spell a Spelling Word.

Example: g __ i n __ p q __ s m __ o *horn*

7. r __ t d __ f q __ s u __ w d __ f _____

8. g __ i d __ f q __ s _____

9. v __ x n __ p q __ s j __ l _____

10. f __ h h __ j q __ s k __ m _____

11. v __ x n __ p q __ s c __ e _____

12. g __ i t __ v q __ s s __ u _____

Name _____

Proofreading and Writing

Proofreading Circle the four misspelled Spelling
Words below. Then write each word correctly.

Here is a good way to reach Barletta.
Head noarth from Naples. At the edge of
town, turn right onto the main highway. This
road should be pretty cleer. Take the therd exit
after you reach the coast. You should get to
Barletta before darck.

Spelling Words

1. girl
2. clear
3. her
4. turn
5. dark
6. work
7. smart
8. word
9. hurt
10. serve
11. north
12. third

_____ _____

_____ _____

Write a Description If you were to make a statue, who would
be your subject? Where would it stand so others could see it?

**On a separate sheet of paper, write a description of your
statue. Tell where it will be placed. Use Spelling Words
from the list.**

Theme 3: **Incredible Stories**   165

Which Meaning Is Correct?

From the definitions below, choose the correct meaning for the underlined word in each sentence. Write the number of the meaning in the blank provided.

---

bargain *noun* **1.** An agreement between two sides; deal: *We made a bargain to split the chores.* **2.** Something offered or bought at a low price: *The book was a bargain at 25 cents.*

---

hail *verb* **1.** To greet or welcome by calling out: *We hailed our friends as they got off the bus.* **2.** To call or signal to: *I hailed a taxi at the corner* **3.** To congratulate by cheering: *The crowd hailed the hero's return.*

---

settle *verb* **1.** To arrange or decide upon: *Let's settle the argument today.* **2.** To come to rest: *The leaf settled on the grass.* **3.** To make a home or place to live in: *Pioneers settled on the prairie.*

---

1. Every day, the townspeople <u>hailed</u> the Mysterious Giant as they walked to the market. _____

2. They asked the statue to help them find a good <u>bargain</u> at the market. _____

3. Doves flew to the statue and <u>settled</u> on his head. _____

4. The Mysterious Giant was <u>hailed</u> as a hero. _____

Name _____

Circling Verbs

Circle the verb in each sentence.

1. The giant statue stands in the center of town.

2. People often look at the statue.

3. Everyone loves the statue.

4. Zia Concetta is the oldest person in Barletta.

5. One day, an enemy army approaches the town.

6. Everyone fears the army of powerful soldiers.

7. The soldiers march toward the town.

8. The mysterious statue hops off his pedestal.

9. He asks for three special things.

10. The giant statue cries because of the onion's smell.

Name _____

Finding Verbs

Find the verb in each sentence, and write it on the line at the right.

1. In this story, the giant statue leaps off its pedestal. _____

2. The people believe in the giant. _____

3. Clearly, the giant cares about the town of Barletta. _____

4. Unfortunately, an army attacks the town. _____

5. The people quickly identify the trouble. _____

6. With a little thought, the giant solves the problem. _____

7. He cuts an onion into two pieces. _____

8. The tears run down his face. _____

9. The army fears the giant and his friends. _____

10. At the end of the story, the soldiers leave town. _____

Use this chart to classify the verbs from the sentences above.

Physical Action	Mental Action
_____	_____
_____	_____
_____	_____
_____	_____

Name _____

Using Exact Verbs

**Circle the verb in each sentence. Then think of an
exact verb to make the sentence more interesting.
Rewrite the sentence using your exact verb.**

1. An army of powerful soldiers appears.

   _____

2. One night, Zia Concetta goes to the statue.

   _____

3. The giant statue moves off the pedestal.

   _____

4. The statue's clever plan beats the large army.

   _____

5. Today, the statue still is in Barletta, Italy.

   _____

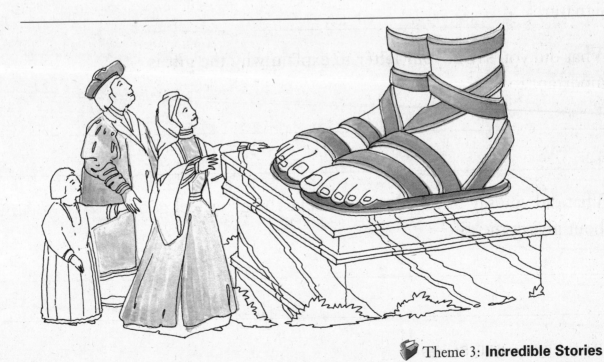

Name _____

Write a Thank-You Note

Use this outline to write a thank-you letter for a gift you have been given. When you have finished your letter, answer the questions below.

Address/Date _____

_____

_____

Greeting _____

Body _____

_____

_____

_____

Closing _____

Signature _____

What did you say in your letter to explain why the gift is important to you?

_____

_____

What did you say in your letter to make the giver feel good about giving the gift?

_____

_____

Name _____

Using Commas for Direct Address

What if in all the excitement at Barletta, no one remembered to thank the vegetable store owner for supplying the very important onion?

Suppose that the thank-you note has now been written, but it needs proofreading. Read the note. Add commas where they belong, before or after the name of the person being addressed.

Dear Sir,

 We the people of Barletta thank you for supplying the onion that made our giant cry! Sir without your onion, our whole plan might have failed miserably. We were ready to run from Barletta, but you Sir stayed bravely in your shop, guarding your vegetables. When your city needed you, you were ready Sir. When we said, "Sir find us an onion," you knew just what to do. Now everyone will always say that it was because of you and your onion that Barletta was saved. Sir you have reason to be proud!

 Sincerely,
 The Mayor

Name _____

Farm Words

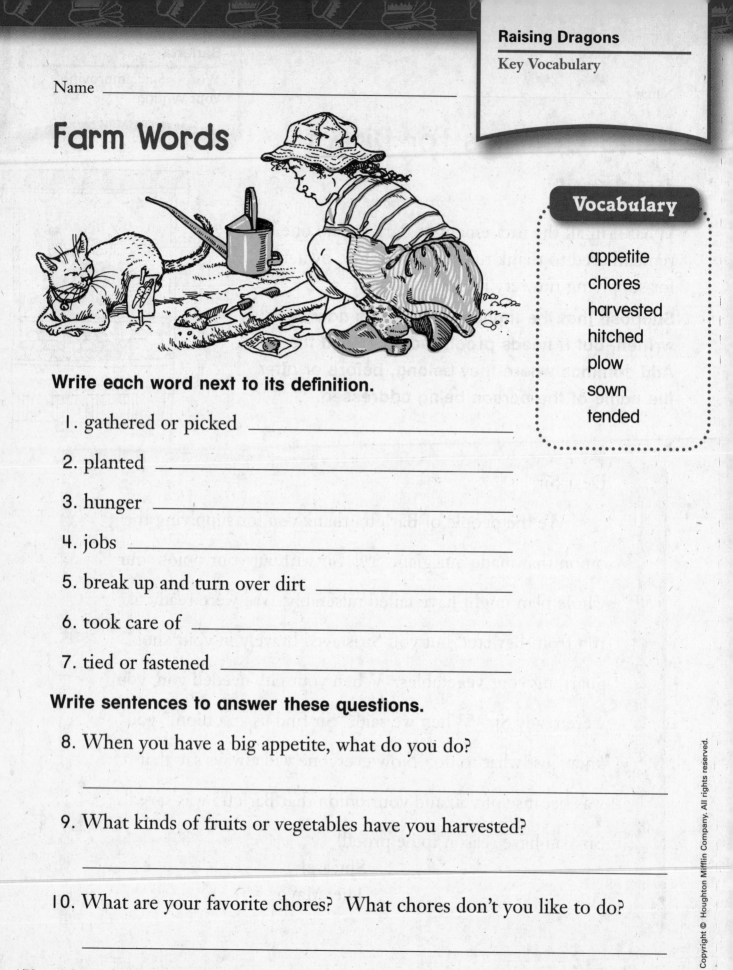

appetite
chores
harvested
hitched
plow
sown
tended

Write each word next to its definition.

1. gathered or picked _____

2. planted _____

3. hunger _____

4. jobs _____

5. break up and turn over dirt _____

6. took care of _____

7. tied or fastened _____

Write sentences to answer these questions.

8. When you have a big appetite, what do you do?

_____

9. What kinds of fruits or vegetables have you harvested?

_____

10. What are your favorite chores? What chores don't you like to do?

_____

Name _____

Conclusions Chart

Story Details		Story Details		Conclusion
(page 320) Pa raises corn, peas, barley, wheat, and many farm animals.	**+**	(Page 320) _____ _____ _____ _____	**=**	Pa _____ _____
(page 323; it's not a rock.) _____ _____	**+**	(page 325) _____ _____ _____	**=**	(What's in Miller's Cave) _____ _____
(page 328; Hank's size) _____ _____	**+**	(Page 328) _____ _____ _____	**=**	(What Hank looks like) _____ _____
(page 334) _____ _____	**+**	(page 337) _____ _____	**=**	(Hank's fate) _____ _____

Name _____

The Dragon's Tale

Tell what happened in *Raising Dragons*.
Complete each sentence to finish the story.

One day a little girl found what looked like a big rock. It was

an egg. She kept wondering _____

_____ .

One night she heard _____ .

Then the little girl saw _____ .

Of course, the girl loved Hank. Each day she fed him and

_____ .

Soon he was part of their lives.

Hank helped around the farm. He saved Ma's tomatoes. He

also saved the corn by _____

_____ .

Then Hank got too much attention. So the girl took Hank to

_____ . She knew

Hank could live there because _____

_____ .

But Hank surprised the little girl with _____

_____ .

Name _____

Conclusions from Clues

Read these details about dragons. Then fill in the chart on the next page.

What Dragons Are Really Like

► Dragons have skin much like snakes, lizards, and other reptiles. Since they are cold-blooded, dragons like to live in warm spots.

► Each spring, dragons lay eggs in nests they build. Their nests are made from the same materials that birds use.

► Dragons can fly, but their wings are not at all like birds' wings. They are more like large, leathery bat wings.

► Usually, dragons will not harm people. They only eat frogs, bugs, and fish. Some dragons have been trained to be useful. They pull plows and do other tasks that horses do.

► Dragons do not breathe fire. However, their teeth are larger than a shark's, and they will use them to keep their babies safe.

Name _____

Conclusions from Clues continued

Read each conclusion. Decide if it is correct, and write YES or NO. Write the clues that helped you decide.

Conclusions	Correct Conclusion? (Yes or No)	Story Clues
Dragon skin is scaly.	_____	
Dragon nests are made of twigs, sticks, and grasses.	_____	
Dragon wings have feathers.	_____	
Dragons can be trained to carry riders.	_____	
Dragons never bite.	_____	

Name ______________________________

Happy Endings

Choose a word from the box to match each picture clue.
Write the word on the line.

Word Bank

proudly	brightly	leaky	cloudy	beastly
furry	lovely	bumpy	rainy	hairy

1.  + y = ___ ___ ___ ___ ___

2.  + ly = ___ ___ ___ ___ ___ ___ ___ ___

3.  + y = ___ ___ ___ ___ ___ ___

4.  + ly = ___ ___ ___ ___ ___ ___ ___

5.  + y = ___ ___ ___ ___ ___

6.  + ly = ___ ___ ___ ___ ___ ___

Name _____

The /j/, /k/, and /kw/ Sounds

► The /j/ sound can be spelled with the consonant *j* or with the consonant *g* followed by *e* or *y*.

    /j/ **j**eans, lar**ge**, **gy**m

► The starred word *judge* has two /j/ sounds in it. The first /j/ sound is spelled *j*, and the second is spelled *dge*.

► The /k/ sound can be spelled with *k*, *ck*, or *c*. The /kw/ sounds can be spelled with the *qu* pattern.

    /k/ par**k**, qui**ck**, pi**c**nic   /kw/ **squ**eeze

1. large
2. gym
3. skin
4. quick
5. picnic
6. judge
7. park
8. jeans
9. crack
10. orange
11. second
12. squeeze

Write the Spelling Words that have the /j/ sound in them. Then write the Spelling Words that have the /k/ or /kw/ sounds in them.

/j/ Sound

_____

_____

_____

_____

/k/ or /kw/ Sounds

_____

_____

_____

_____

_____

Name _____

Spelling Spree

Silly Rhymes Write a Spelling Word to complete each sentence. The answer rhymes with the underlined word.

Spelling Words

1. large
2. gym
3. skin
4. quick
5. picnic
6. judge
7. park
8. jeans
9. crack
10. orange
11. second
12. squeeze

1. The hungry _____ ate some <u>fudge</u>.

2. Birds in the _____ sleep after <u>dark</u>.

3. I dropped baked <u>beans</u> on my new _____ .

4. There is a _____ in the train <u>track</u>.

5. Can more <u>bees</u> _____ into the hive?

6. A _____ <u>barge</u> is on the river.

1. _____   4. _____

2. _____   5. _____

3. _____   6. _____

Letter Math Solve each problem by using a Spelling Word.

> **Example:** joke – ke + b = *job*

7. pick – k + nic = _____

8. or + angel – l = _____

9. s + king – g = _____

10. quit – t + ck = _____

11. sec + fond – f = _____

12. edgy – ed + m = _____

Theme 3: **Incredible Stories**   179

Name _____

Proofreading and Writing

Proofreading Circle the five misspelled Spelling Words. Then write each word correctly.

Dear Diary,

Today we went to the zoo. We saw larje snakes and turtles. One turtle splashed water on my geans! There was a dragon cage, but it was empty. I guess the dragons were taking a quik nap inside. For lunch we had a picnick. I ate mine in the parc.

1. large
2. gym
3. skin
4. quick
5. picnic
6. judge
7. park
8. jeans
9. crack
10. orange
11. second
12. squeeze

1. _____
2. _____
3. _____
4. _____
5. _____

Write a List of Rules A baby dragon would need a lot of care. What rules should someone follow when raising a dragon?

On a separate sheet of paper, write a list of rules for taking care of a dragon. Use Spelling Words from the list.

Name _____

Say It Right!

Pronunciation Key			
ă map	ĭ pit	oi **oil**	th ba**th**
ā pay	ī ride	ŏŏ b**oo**k	*th* ba**the**
â care	î f**ie**rce	o͞o b**oo**t	ə **a**go, it**e**m,
ä father	ŏ pot	ou **out**	penc**i**l, at**o**m,
ĕ pet	ō go	ŭ cup	circ**u**s
ē be	ô paw, for	û fur	

**Look at the vowel sound in the words below. Then look at
the Pronunciation Key and find the sample word with the
same vowel sound. Write the word on the line.**

1. **must** (mŭst) _____

2. **dirt** (dûrt) _____

3. **breath** (brĕth) _____

4. **path** (păth) _____

5. **chew** (cho͞o) _____

6. **self** (sĕlf) _____

7. **dear** (dîr) _____

8. **pair** (pâr) _____

9. **meal** (mîl) _____

10. **stay** (stā) _____

Name _____

Looking for the Present

Read each sentence. Choose the correct verb form and write it on the line to complete the sentence.

1. This story _____ about a girl and her pet dragon. (tell   tells)

2. The dog _____ when it sees the giant egg. (barks   bark)

3. The neighbors _____ the egg hatching. (watch   watches)

4. A large claw _____ from inside the egg. (appear   appears)

5. The girl _____ the newborn dragon. (dry   dries)

6. The strange pet _____ when he sees the girl. (smiles   smile)

7. Her parents _____ about owning a dragon. (worries   worry)

8. Dragons _____ fire. (breathe   breathes)

9. The dragon _____ with the girl on his back. (flies fly)

10. Clouds _____ the two flying friends. (surround   surrounds)

Name _____

Choosing the Present

Read each sentence. Then write the correct present-time form of the verb in parentheses.

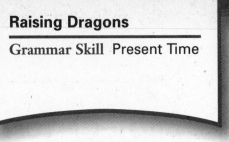

1. A smart girl _____ a pet dragon. (raise)

2. The chickens _____ when they see the baby dragon. (cluck)

3. All animals _____ to eat. (need)

4. This dragon _____ on fish, frogs, eels, and insects. (munch)

5. The strange creature _____ to be a good friend. (try)

6. The friends _____ the farm together. (cross)

7. The dragon _____ with daily chores. (help)

8. His hot breath _____ the corn in the field. (pop)

9. Customers _____ the dragon's popcorn. (buy)

10. The girl _____ when the dragon leaves. (cry)

Name _____

Subject-Verb Agreement

**Proofread these paragraphs. Correct
errors in subject-verb agreement.
Circle verbs that are not in the correct time.
Then rewrite the paragraphs on the lines provided.**

    Benjamin wakes at sunrise. He look outside his apartment
window. At first, he see only the sun. Then he spot five black dots
in the distance. The dots grows bigger and bigger. Suddenly, Ben's
jaw drop wide open. Five big black dragons flies outside his window.

    The dragons calls to Benjamin. "Come fly with us!" they shout.
Benjamin think about it. In a few seconds, he decide. In a flash, he
jump onto one of the dragons. The new friends zooms into the air.
Benjamin laughs and wonder what will happen next.

_____

_____

_____

_____

_____

_____

_____

Name _____

Planning Your Writing

Use this page to plan your opinion. Then number your reasons or facts in the order you will use them.

Topic: _____

Topic Sentence: _____

Reason/Fact:	Reason/Fact:

Reason/Fact:	Reason/Fact:

Name _____

Using Commas with Introductory Phrases

Select the introductory group of words from the box that best completes each sentence.

for example	first of all	in addition
in conclusion	most important	

Cats Are the Best Pets

I think cats are the best pets. (1)

_____ they are fun to watch.

(2) _____ if you roll a ball in

front of it, a cat will bat it around the house.

(3) _____ cats like to play with

string for hours. (4) _____ cats

are good companions. They follow you around the house,

and they sleep in your lap. (5) _____

those are the reasons why I think cats are the best pets!

Name _____

A Garden of Words

**Circle the word that best completes each sentence.
Then write the word in the blank.**

1. The elephants were so large they were _____ .
   A. impossible   C. awesome
   B. weak   D. smart

2. My teacher _____ me that some
   kinds of plants can eat insects.
   A. discovered   C. rewarded
   B. disappeared D. convinced

3. I saw a bird in a tree, but it flew off and _____ .
   A. disappeared C. grew
   B. discovered   D. walked

4. In the pond, I _____ a frog that
   looked like a leaf.
   A. thought   C. convinced
   B. discovered   D. read

5. We thought the lion's loud roar was _____ .
   A. quiet   C. incredible
   B. tiny   D. impossible

6. It was almost _____ to see

   the white polar bear sitting in the white snow.
   A. best   C. incredible
   B. awesome   D. impossible

Name _____

Story Map

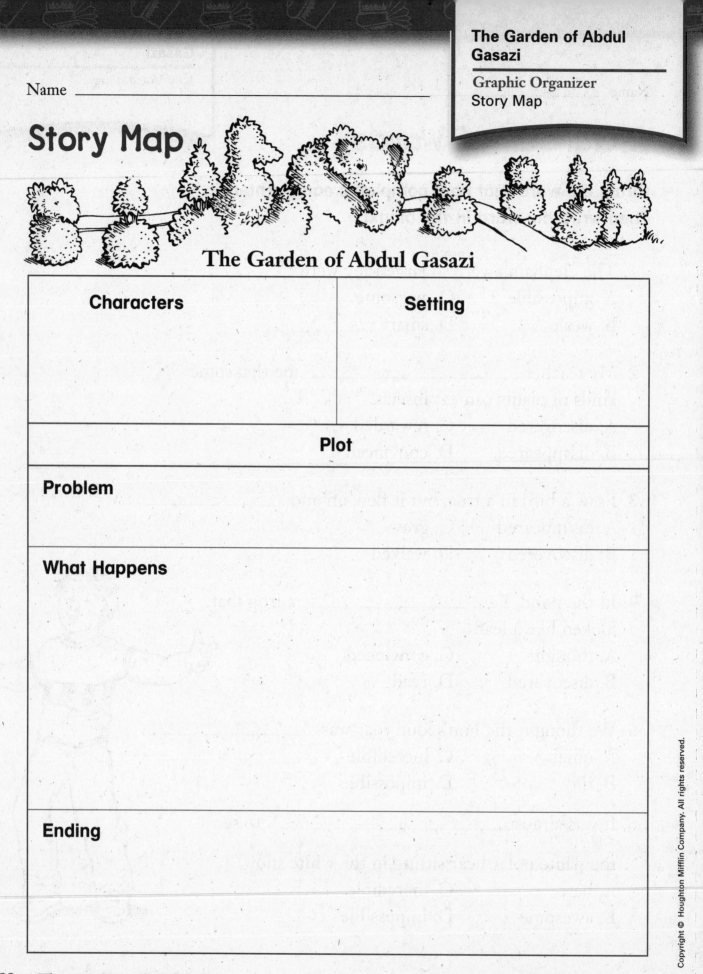

The Garden of Abdul Gasazi

Characters	Setting

Plot

Problem

What Happens

Ending

Name _____

Mr. Gasazi's Garden!

Complete each sentence with an event from
The Garden of Abdul Gasazi. **Then explain how**
you feel about the way the story ends.

1. Miss Hester must visit Cousin Eunice, so she asks

   _____

2. When Alan takes Fritz for a walk,

   _____

3. As Alan searches for Fritz, he finds _____

4. The magician tells Alan that he has _____

   _____

5. As Alan leaves, _____

6. When Alan returns to Miss Hester's, Fritz _____

   _____

7. Miss Hester tells Alan that _____

8. After Alan leaves, Miss Hester tells Fritz that he is a bad dog

   because _____

   ### My Feelings About the Ending:

   _____

   _____

The Shape of a Story

Read the story below.

Rescuing Dolly

One cold morning as Keisha walked her dog, Vista, she noticed fresh tracks in the snow. A minute later, a small, spotted dog appeared by the river. With no tag or collar, it clearly was lost. It stared hopefully at Keisha and shivered in the cold. Then Vista barked, and the dog ran off. "It's much too cold for a dog to stay outside for long," Keisha thought. "I've got to do something, but Vista will keep scaring it away."

So Keisha headed for home. She told her mother about the lost dog, and together they returned to the river to find it.

Keisha was almost ready to give up, but at last she spotted the dog. Keisha called to it, but it jumped onto a rock. Then Keisha knelt down. The little dog leaped into her arms and began licking her face.

Weeks later, the little dog's owner still could not be found. So that is how Dolly, the little dog, came to be part of Keisha's family.

Name _____

The Shape of a Story continued

Fill in this story map with details from "Rescuing Dolly."

Characters	Setting
1. _____	
2. _____	

Plot
Problem
_____
What Happens
1. _____
2. _____
3. _____
4. _____
Ending
1. _____
2. _____

Name _____

Playing with Prefixes

On each line, write a word that begins with the
prefix *un-, dis-,* or *non-* and matches the definition.
Then find and circle all eight words in the word search.

1. not locked _____

2. not fiction _____

3. the opposite of agree _____

4. not able _____

5. the opposite of appear _____

6. not usual _____

7. not fair _____

8. not making sense _____

```
K N O N F I C T I O N D A D F P E P
D E R W H Y N E Z G Q J X H G H T V
I Z W U C Q X U S Y C Y S S V M Z C
S T V A N L N O N S E N S E Z P G Z
A N P K A L M B S U I G I V K A O R
P V N O W J O O D G S P H Q M H M Z
P T G J G Z O C R S S U U N F A I R
E R Y X W L P F K X M P A Z H Z A R
A H E R J Q M W M E G V T L M O J E
R E U N A B L E L P D I S A G R E E
```

Name _____

Homophones

Homophones are words that sound the same but have different spellings and meanings. When you spell a homophone, think about the meaning of the word you want to write.

Homophone	Meaning
/n$\overline{oo}$/ **new**	not old
/n$\overline{oo}$/ **kn**ew	understood

Write the four pairs of Spelling Words that are homophones.

_____   _____

_____   _____

_____   _____

_____   _____

Now write the three Spelling Words that are homophones.

_____

_____

_____

Spelling Words

1. hear
2. here
3. new
4. knew
5. its
6. it's
7. our
8. hour
9. there
10. their
11. they're

Name _____

Spelling Spree

Quotation Caper Write the Spelling Word that best
completes each quotation that might have come
from the story.

1. "We magicians never reveal _____
   secrets," said Mr. Gasazi.

2. "Your hat is not in _____ usual place,"
   said Miss Hester.

3. "The ducks have flown back to _____
   pond," said Alan.

4. "Fritz, come back _____ !" called Alan.

5. "Dogs should know that _____ not
   welcome here," grumbled Gasazi.

1. _____	4. _____
2. _____	5. _____
3. _____	

Spelling Words

1. hear
2. here
3. new
4. knew
5. its
6. it's
7. our
8. hour
9. there
10. their
11. they're

In Another Word Write a Spelling Word
to replace each expression.

6. get wind of   _____

7. hot off the press   _____

8. over yonder   _____

9. got the picture   _____

Name _____

Proofreading and Writing

Proofreading Suppose that Alan keeps a journal.
Circle the five misspelled Spelling Words
in this entry. Then write each word correctly.

Spelling Words

1. hear
2. here
3. new
4. knew
5. its
6. it's
7. our
8. hour
9. there
10. their
11. they're

June 3: Today I had a strange adventure. It was in a magician's garden. Miss Hester's dog Fritz ran in their. I knue we were in trouble when I read the sign: "No dogs allowed." I chased Fritz for at least an our. I think its' possible that the magician turned Fritz into a duck! When I came back heere, no one believed my story.

1. _____
2. _____
3. _____
4. _____
5. _____

Write a Plan Abdul Gasazi had some amazing trees in his garden. If you could plan a garden, what would you plant in it? Where would you plant things?

On a separate sheet of paper, draw a picture of your garden. Then write a plan for it. Tell what you would plant, and where. Use Spelling Words from the list.

grass

pool

Trees

Ask Your Friendly Thesaurus!

For each underlined word in the following sentences, choose a better word or words from the thesaurus entry. Write your answers in the blanks provided. Some words may have more than one answer.

Thesaurus Entries

1. **funny:** silly, unusual, curious, laughable
2. **pulled:** strained, dragged, stretched, heaved
3. **ran:** darted, flowed, fled, hurried
4. **tired:** exhausted, faint, worn, wilting
5. **walking:** strolling, trotting, striding, stomping
6. **shouted:** called, bellowed, howled, bawled

1. Fritz stopped chewing the furniture and fell asleep,

   completely <u>tired</u>. _____

2. Alan fastened Fritz's leash and the dog <u>pulled</u> him out of

   the house. _____

3. Fritz <u>ran</u> straight through the open door.

   _____

4. Gasazi <u>shouted</u> that he had turned the dogs into ducks!

   _____

5. Alan felt <u>funny</u> when he thought the magician had fooled

   him. _____

6. Fritz came <u>walking</u> up the front steps with Alan's hat.

   _____

Name _____

Choosing Time

Choose the correct verb form in parentheses and write it on the line provided to complete the sentence.

1. Tomorrow Alan _____ Fritz for a walk. (takes   will take)

2. Yesterday Alan _____ for Fritz. (searched   will search)

3. Yesterday in the garden, Fritz _____ into Abdul. (bumped   will bump)

4. Tomorrow Alan _____ the stairs. (climbed   will climb)

5. Yesterday the ducks _____ their wings. (flapped   will flap)

Complete the chart by supplying past and future time for each of the verbs given.

Verb	Past Time	Future Time
try	_____	_____
race	_____	_____
disappear	_____	_____
drag	_____	_____
bolt	_____	_____

Name _____

Writing Past and Future

Read each sentence. Then write the sentence in past time and future time.

1. Alan walks Fritz.

   Past: _____

   Future: _____

2. He hurries after the dog.

   Past: _____

   Future: _____

3. Alan discovers the magician.

   Past: _____

   Future: _____

4. Abdul shows Alan a duck.

   Past: _____

   Future: _____

5. The duck grabs Alan's hat.

   Past: _____

   Future: _____

198   Theme 3: **Incredible Stories**

Name _____

Keeping Verbs Consistent

Read this story. The paragraphs mix up the past, the present, and the future. The story takes place in the past. Circle any verbs that are not in past time. Then write the verbs correctly on the lines below.

I visited a strange garden yesterday. The bushes look like different animals. A giant green elephant watches the main path. I discovered a hidden path. I will follow the trail.

A strange noise sounds behind me. I turned around. The elephant moves! Then the giant plant faces in the other direction.

I decide to leave the weird garden. I try to find my way out. I looked everywhere. The paths twisted and turned.

I turn around again. The elephant watches me. I step farther into the garden. The elephant stared.

Finally, I uncover a hidden gate. I hurry toward it. The elephant appears in front of me. I raced out of the garden. Then I glance back. The garden is gone.

_____ _____ _____

_____ _____ _____

_____ _____ _____

_____ _____ _____

Theme 3: **Incredible Stories**   199

Name _____

Writing Dialogue

Write a dialogue, or a conversation between two or more characters in a story. Try to make the dialogue sound as if real people are talking. Use quotation marks, capital letters, and commas in your dialogue. Choose one of the following groups of characters for your dialogue:

▶ Alan and Miss Hester
▶ Alan and Abdul Gasazi
▶ Miss Hester and Abdul Gasazi
▶ Alan, Miss Hester, and Abdul Gasazi
▶ Two characters from another story of your choice

_____

_____

_____

_____

_____

_____

_____

_____

_____

_____

Name _____

Write Quotations Right!

Rewrite each of the following sentences of dialogue  that might have taken place. Add quotation marks, capital letters, or commas.

1. Miss Hester said please stay with Fritz and give him his afternoon walk.

_____

_____

2. don't chew on the furniture, Fritz Alan said angrily.

_____

_____

3. please, Fritz Alan exclaimed don't go running off into that garden!

_____

_____

4. Alan said if you have Fritz, Mr. Gasazi, would you please give him back?

_____

_____

5. something terrible has happened, Miss Hester Alan blurted out. your dog ran away, and Mr. Gasazi turned him into a duck!

_____

_____

Name _____

Writing a Personal Response

Use the test-taking strategies and tips you have learned to help you answer this kind of question. Take the time you need to decide which topic you will write about and to write an answer. Then read your response and see how you may make it better. This practice will help you when you take this kind of test.

Write one or two paragraphs about one of the following topics.

a. You have read *The Mysterious Giant of Barletta*. If you could choose a statue or something else to come to life, what would it be? Tell why you would choose it and how it might act.

b. Zia Concetta said *"grazie"* (thank you) to the Mysterious Giant. In what other ways do you think the townspeople could thank the Giant? How do you thank people for nice things they have done for you?

_____

_____

_____

_____

_____

_____

_____

_____

Name _____

Writing a Personal Response

continued

Read your answer. Check to be sure that it

■ sticks to the topic.

■ is well organized.

■ has details that support your answer.

■ has vivid and exact words.

■ has few mistakes in capitalization, punctuation, grammar, or spelling.

Now pick one way you can improve your response.
Make your changes below.

_____

_____

_____

_____

_____

_____

_____

_____

_____

_____

_____

_____

_____

Name _____

Spelling Review

**Write each Spelling Word. Then circle six words that
are homophone pairs.**

1. _____
2. _____
3. _____
4. _____
5. _____
6. _____
7. _____
8. _____
9. _____
10. _____
11. _____
12. _____
13. _____
14. _____
15. _____
16. _____
17. _____
18. _____
19. _____
20. _____
21. _____
22. _____
23. _____
24. _____
25. _____

Spelling Words

1. word
2. sound
3. clear
4. also
5. soft
6. crack
7. lawn
8. crown
9. girl
10. knew
11. here
12. turn
13. dark
14. north
15. orange
16. her
17. skin
18. hear
19. squeeze
20. gym
21. second
22. jeans
23. hour
24. our
25. new

Name _____

Spelling Spree

Puzzle Play Write a Spelling Word for each clue.
Then use the letters in the boxes to spell a word
about what a dragon is like.

1. this covers your body ☐ ___ ___ ___

2. first, —, third ___ ___ ☐ ___ ___ ___

3. heavy blue pants ___ ___ ☐ ___ ___

4. 60 minutes ___ ___ ☐ ___

5. a large indoor play area ___ ☐ ___

Secret Word: _____

Picture Clues Write Spelling
Words for each sentence.

6–7. The _____ is holding an

_____ .

8–9. Stones from the _____ in

the wall are lying on the _____ .

10–12. The king, wearing his _____ ,

cannot _____ the soft

_____ .

Spelling Words

1. sound
2. lawn
3. crown
4. girl
5. skin
6. crack
7. gym
8. orange
9. second
10. jeans
11. hear
12. hour

Name _____

Proofreading and Writing

Proofreading Circle the five misspelled Spelling Words below. Write each word correctly.

> It can be lonely hear in my big house. I don't hear a werd from morning until darc. This morning, however, I heard a saft sound. It was my friend Masha, who held out a hand for me to skweeze.

Spelling Words
1. clear
2. girl
3. turn
4. also
5. squeeze
6. dark
7. soft
8. north
9. her
10. new
11. here
12. our
13. knew
14. word

1. _____   4. _____

2. _____   5. _____

3. _____

Which Word? Write the Spelling Word that best fits each group of words.

6. understood or _____   11. opposite of south _____

7. unused or _____   12. boy and _____

8. in addition _____   13. to spin, circle, or _____

9. sunny and _____   14. we, us, _____

10. his or her _____

Write Directions On another sheet of paper, write directions telling the giant how to get from your school to your house. Use the Spelling Review Words.

Theme 3: **Incredible Stories**   207

Student Handbook

Contents

How to Study a Word

1. LOOK at the word.
- ► What does the word mean?
- ► What letters are in the word?
- ► Name and touch each letter.

2. SAY the word.
- ► Listen for the consonant sounds.
- ► Listen for the vowel sounds.

3. THINK about the word.
- ► How is each sound spelled?
- ► Close your eyes and picture the word.
- ► What familiar spelling patterns do you see?
- ► What other words have the same spelling patterns?

4. WRITE the word.
- ► Think about the sounds and the letters.
- ► Form the letters correctly.

5. CHECK the spelling.
- ► Did you spell the word the same way it is spelled in your word list?
- ► If you did not spell the word correctly, write the word again.

about	don't	I'd		
again	down	I'll		
almost		I'm	outside	tonight
a lot	enough	into		too
also	every	its	people	two
always	everybody	it's	pretty	
am				until
and	family	January	really	
another	favorite		right	very
anyone	February	knew		
anyway	field	know	said	want
around	finally		Saturday	was
	for	letter	school	Wednesday
beautiful	found	like	some	we're
because	friend	little	something	where
been	from	lose	started	while
before		lying	stopped	who
brought	getting		sure	whole
buy	girl	might	swimming	world
	goes	morning		would
cannot	going	mother	than	wouldn't
can't	guess	myself	that's	write
clothes			their	writing
coming	happily	never	them	
could	have	new	then	you
cousin	haven't	now	there	your
	heard		they	
does	her	off	thought	
didn't	here	one	through	
different	his	other	to	
done	how	our	today	

The Ballad of Mulan

More Short Vowels

/ŏ/ → lot
/ŭ/ → rub

Spelling Words

1. pond
2. luck
3. drop
4. lot
5. rub
6. does
7. drum
8. sock
9. hunt
10. crop
11. shut
12. won

Challenge Words

1. dodge
2. dusk

My Study List
Add your own spelling words on the back. ➡

Off to Adventure!
Reading-Writing Workshop

Look for familiar spelling patterns in these words to help you remember their spellings.

Spelling Words

1. have
2. haven't
3. found
4. around
5. one
6. than
7. then
8. them
9. before
10. because
11. other
12. mother

Challenge Words

1. family
2. cousin
3. everybody
4. guess

My Study List
Add your own spelling words on the back. ➡

The Lost and Found

Short Vowels

/ă/ → last
/ĕ/ → smell
/ĭ/ → mix

Spelling Words

1. mix
2. milk
3. smell
4. last
5. head
6. friend
7. class
8. left
9. thick
10. send
11. thin
12. stick

Challenge Words

1. empty
2. glance

My Study List
Add your own spelling words on the back. ➡

Take-Home Word List

Take-Home Word List

Take-Home Word List

Name _____

Name _____

Name _____

My Study List

1. _____
2. _____
3. _____
4. _____
5. _____
6. _____
7. _____
8. _____
9. _____
10. _____

Review Words

1. test
2. dish

My Study List

1. _____
2. _____
3. _____
4. _____
5. _____
6. _____
7. _____
8. _____
9. _____
10. _____

My Study List

1. _____
2. _____
3. _____
4. _____
5. _____
6. _____
7. _____
8. _____
9. _____
10. _____

Review Words

1. hop
2. much

How to Study a Word

Look at the word.
Say the word.
Think about the word.
Write the word.
Check the spelling.

How to Study a Word

Look at the word.
Say the word.
Think about the word.
Write the word.
Check the spelling.

How to Study a Word

Look at the word.
Say the word.
Think about the word.
Write the word.
Check the spelling.

The Keeping Quilt

More Long Vowel Spellings

| /ā/ | ➡ | paint, clay |
| /ē/ | ➡ | leave, feel |

Spelling Words

1. paint
2. clay
3. feel
4. leave
5. neighbor
6. eight
7. seem
8. speak
9. paid
10. lay
11. need
12. weigh

Challenge Words

1. needle
2. crayon

My Study List
Add your own spelling words on the back. ➡

Off to Adventure!
Spelling Review
Spelling Words

1. last
2. mix
3. stick
4. lot
5. sock
6. hunt
7. wide
8. grade
9. thick
10. send
11. class
12. pond
13. luck
14. drum
15. save
16. cube
17. smile
18. left
19. smell
20. thin
21. drop
22. shut
23. huge
24. note
25. life

See the back for Challenge Words.

My Study List
Add your own spelling words on the back. ➡

The Waterfall

The Vowel-Consonant-e Pattern

/ā/	➡	save
/ī/	➡	life
/ō/	➡	smoke
/yōō/	➡	huge

Spelling Words

1. smoke
2. huge
3. save
4. life
5. wide
6. come
7. mine
8. grade
9. smile
10. note
11. cube
12. love

Challenge Words

1. escape
2. slope

My Study List
Add your own spelling words on the back. ➡

Take-Home Word List

Take-Home Word List

Take-Home Word List

Name _____

Name _____

Name _____

My Study List

1. _____
2. _____
3. _____
4. _____
5. _____
6. _____
7. _____
8. _____
9. _____
10. _____

Review Words

1. side
2. hope

My Study List

1. _____
2. _____
3. _____
4. _____
5. _____
6. _____
7. _____
8. _____
9. _____
10. _____

Challenge Words

1. glance
2. empty
3. dusk
4. slope
5. escape

My Study List

1. _____
2. _____
3. _____
4. _____
5. _____
6. _____
7. _____
8. _____
9. _____
10. _____

Review Words

1. clean
2. play

How to Study a Word

Look at the word.
Say the word.
Think about the word.
Write the word.
Check the spelling.

How to Study a Word

Look at the word.
Say the word.
Think about the word.
Write the word.
Check the spelling.

How to Study a Word

Look at the word.
Say the word.
Think about the word.
Write the word.
Check the spelling.

The Talking Cloth

**Three-Letter Clusters
and Unexpected
Consonant Patterns**
spring
street
throw
/n/ ➞ knee
/r/ ➞ wrap
/ch/ ➞ watch

Spelling Words

1. spring
2. knee
3. throw
4. patch
5. strong
6. wrap
7. three
8. watch
9. street
10. know
11. spread
12. write

Challenge Words

1. strength
2. kitchen

My Study List
Add your own
spelling words
on the back. ➡

217

Anthony Reynoso: Born to Rope

The Long o Sound
/ō/ ➞ coach,
blow, hold

Spelling Words

1. coach
2. blow
3. float
4. hold
5. sew
6. though
7. sold
8. soap
9. row
10. own
11. both
12. most

Challenge Words

1. tomorrow
2. program

My Study List
Add your own
spelling words
on the back. ➡

217

Celebrating Traditions
Reading-Writing Workshop

Look for familiar
spelling patterns in
these words to help
you remember their
spellings.

Spelling Words

1. now
2. off
3. for
4. almost
5. also
6. can't
7. cannot
8. about
9. always
10. today
11. until
12. again

Challenge Words

1. February
2. January
3. Saturday
4. Wednesday

My Study List
Add your own
spelling words
on the back. ➡

217

Name _____

My Study List

1. _____
2. _____
3. _____
4. _____
5. _____
6. _____
7. _____
8. _____
9. _____
10. _____

Name _____

My Study List

1. _____
2. _____
3. _____
4. _____
5. _____
6. _____
7. _____
8. _____
9. _____
10. _____

Review Words

1. cold
2. slow

Name _____

My Study List

1. _____
2. _____
3. _____
4. _____
5. _____
6. _____
7. _____
8. _____
9. _____
10. _____

Review Words

1. catch
2. two

How to Study a Word

Look at the word.
Say the word.
Think about the word.
Write the word.
Check the spelling.

How to Study a Word

Look at the word.
Say the word.
Think about the word.
Write the word.
Check the spelling.

How to Study a Word

Look at the word.
Say the word.
Think about the word.
Write the word.
Check the spelling.

Dogzilla

The Vowel Sounds in *clown* and *lawn*

/ou/ → cl**ow**n, s**ou**nd
/ô/ → l**aw**n, cl**o**th, t**a**lk

Spelling Words

1. clown
2. lawn
3. talk
4. sound
5. cloth
6. would
7. also
8. mouth
9. crown
10. soft
11. count
12. law

Challenge Words

1. bounce
2. officer

My Study List
Add your own spelling words on the back. ➡

Celebrating Traditions
Spelling Review

Spelling Words

1. speak
2. feel
3. seem
4. most
5. both
6. know
7. street
8. lie
9. need
10. paint
11. hold
12. float
13. three
14. spread
15. mind
16. might
17. lay
18. leave
19. own
20. row
21. wrap
22. patch
23. tie
24. wild
25. bright

See the back for Challenge Words.

My Study List
Add your own spelling words on the back. ➡

Dancing Rainbows

The Long *i* Sound

/ī/ → br**igh**t, w**i**ld, d**ie**

Spelling Words

1. wild
2. bright
3. die
4. sight
5. child
6. pie
7. fight
8. lie
9. tight
10. tie
11. might
12. mind

Challenge Words

1. design
2. delight

My Study List
Add your own spelling words on the back. ➡

Take-Home Word List

Take-Home Word List

Take-Home Word List

Name _____

My Study List

1. _____
2. _____
3. _____
4. _____
5. _____
6. _____
7. _____
8. _____
9. _____
10. _____

Review Words

1. find
2. high

How to Study a Word

Look at the word.
Say the word.
Think about the word.
Write the word.
Check the spelling.

Name _____

My Study List

1. _____
2. _____
3. _____
4. _____
5. _____
6. _____
7. _____
8. _____
9. _____
10. _____

Challenge Words

1. needle
2. tomorrow
3. program
4. kitchen
5. design

How to Study a Word

Look at the word.
Say the word.
Think about the word.
Write the word.
Check the spelling.

Name _____

My Study List

1. _____
2. _____
3. _____
4. _____
5. _____
6. _____
7. _____
8. _____
9. _____
10. _____

Review Words

1. town
2. small

How to Study a Word

Look at the word.
Say the word.
Think about the word.
Write the word.
Check the spelling.

Raising Dragons

The /j/, /k/, and /kw/ Sounds

/j/ ➡ **j**eans, lar**ge**, **gy**m

/k/ ➡ par**k**, qui**ck**, pi**c**ni**c**

/kw/ ➡ **qu**ick

Spelling Words

1. large
2. gym
3. skin
4. quick
5. picnic
6. judge
7. park
8. jeans
9. crack
10. orange
11. second
12. squeeze

Challenge Words

1. courage
2. insect

My Study List
Add your own spelling words on the back. ➡

The Mysterious Giant of Barletta

Vowel + /r/ Sounds

/är/ ➡ d**ar**k

/î\r/ ➡ cl**ear**

/ôr/ ➡ n**or**th

/ûr/ ➡ h**er**, g**ir**l, t**ur**n, w**or**k

Spelling Words

1. girl
2. clear
3. her
4. turn
5. dark
6. work
7. smart
8. word
9. hurt
10. serve
11. north
12. third

Challenge Words

1. tornado
2. scurried

My Study List
Add your own spelling words on the back. ➡

Incredible Stories

Reading-Writing Workshop

Look for familiar spelling patterns in these words to help you remember their spellings.

Spelling Words

1. and
2. said
3. goes
4. going
5. some
6. something
7. you
8. your
9. friend
10. school
11. where
12. myself

Challenge Words

1. tonight
2. lying
3. field
4. enough

My Study List
Add your own spelling words on the back. ➡

Name _____

My Study List

1. _____
2. _____
3. _____
4. _____
5. _____
6. _____
7. _____
8. _____
9. _____
10. _____

How to Study a Word

Look at the word.
Say the word.
Think about the word.
Write the word.
Check the spelling.

Name _____

My Study List

1. _____
2. _____
3. _____
4. _____
5. _____
6. _____
7. _____
8. _____
9. _____
10. _____

Review Words

1. hard
2. morning

How to Study a Word

Look at the word.
Say the word.
Think about the word.
Write the word.
Check the spelling.

Name _____

My Study List

1. _____
2. _____
3. _____
4. _____
5. _____
6. _____
7. _____
8. _____
9. _____
10. _____

Review Words

1. rock
2. job

How to Study a Word

Look at the word.
Say the word.
Think about the word.
Write the word.
Check the spelling.

Incredible Stories
Spelling Review

Spelling Words

1. sound	14. second
2. crown	15. here
3. word	16. new
4. her	17. soft
5. crack	18. turn
6. orange	19. north
7. hear	20. skin
8. our	21. gym
9. also	22. jeans
10. girl	23. hour
11. dark	24. knew
12. clear	25. lawn
13. squeeze	

**See the back for
Challenge Words**

My Study List
Add your own
spelling words
on the back. ➡

The Garden of
Abdul Gasazi

Homophones
Homophones are
words that sound alike
but have different
spellings and
meanings.

Spelling Words

1. hear
2. here
3. new
4. knew
5. its
6. it's
7. our
8. hour
9. there
10. their
11. they're

Challenge Words
1. seen
2. scene

My Study List
Add your own
spelling words
on the back. ➡

223

223

Name _____

My Study List

1. _____
2. _____
3. _____
4. _____
5. _____
6. _____
7. _____
8. _____
9. _____
10. _____

Review Words

1. eye
2. I

How to Study a Word

Look at the word.
Say the word.
Think about the word.
Write the word.
Check the spelling.

Name _____

My Study List

1. _____
2. _____
3. _____
4. _____
5. _____
6. _____
7. _____
8. _____
9. _____
10. _____

Challenge Words

1. officer
2. scurried
3. insect
4. seen
5. scene

How to Study a Word

Look at the word.
Say the word.
Think about the word.
Write the word.
Check the spelling.

Problem Words

Words	Rules	Examples
are our	*Are* is a verb. *Our* is a possessive pronoun.	<u>Are</u> these gloves yours? This is <u>our</u> car.
doesn't don't	Use *doesn't* with singular nouns, *he*, *she*, and *it*. Use *don't* with plural nouns, *I*, *you*, *we*, and *they*.	Dad <u>doesn't</u> swim. We <u>don't</u> swim.
good well	Use the adjective *good* to describe nouns. Use the adverb *well* to describe verbs.	The weather looks <u>good</u>. She sings <u>well</u>.
its it's	*Its* is a possessive pronoun. *It's* means "it is" (contraction).	The dog wagged <u>its</u> tail. <u>It's</u> cold today.
let leave	*Let* means "to allow." *Leave* means "to go away from" or "to let stay."	Please <u>let</u> me go swimming. I will <u>leave</u> soon. <u>Leave</u> it on my desk.
set sit	*Set* means "to put." *Sit* means "to rest or stay in one place."	<u>Set</u> the vase on the table. Please <u>sit</u> in this chair.
their there they're	*Their* means "belonging to them." *There* means "at or in that place." *They're* means "they are" (contraction).	<u>Their</u> coats are on the bed. Is Carlos <u>there</u>? <u>They're</u> going to the store.
two to too	*Two* is a number *To* means "toward." *Too* means "also" or "more than enough.	I bought <u>two</u> shirts. A cat ran <u>to</u> the tree. Can we go <u>too</u>? I ate <u>too</u> many peas.
your you're	*Your* is a possessive pronoun. *You're* means "you are" (contraction).	Are these <u>your</u> glasses? <u>You're</u> late again!

Proofreading Checklist

Read each question below. Then check your paper. Correct any mistakes you find. After you have corrected them, put a check mark in the box next to the question.

☐ 1. Did I indent each paragraph?

☐ 2. Does each sentence tell one complete thought?

☐ 3. Did I end each sentence with the correct end mark?

☐ 4. Did I begin each sentence with a capital letter?

☐ 5. Did I use capital letters correctly in other places?

☐ 6. Did I use commas correctly?

☐ 7. Did I spell all the words the right way?

Are there other problem areas you should watch for? Make your own proofreading checklist.

☐ _____

☐ _____

☐ _____

☐ _____

☐ _____

☐ _____

☐ _____

Mark	Explanation	Examples
¶	Begin a new paragraph. Indent the paragraph.	¶We went to an air show last Saturday. Eight jets flew across the sky in the shape of V's, X's, and diamonds.
∧	Add letters, words, or sentences.	The leaves were red ∧orange. *and*
℘	Take out words, sentences, and punctuation marks. Correct spelling.	The sky is bright blew. *blue* Huge clouds, move quickly.
/	Change a capital letter to a small letter.	The /Fireflies blinked in the dark.
≡	Change a small letter to a capital letter.	New York city is exciting. ≡

Student Handbook